Writing
Research Papers

Writing
Research
Papers

A Practical Guide

SECOND EDITION

Edward P. Bailey, Jr.
Philip A. Powell

Holt, Rinehart and Winston
New York   Chicago   San Francisco   Philadelphia
Montreal   Toronto   London   Sydney
Tokyo   Mexico City   Rio de Janeiro   Madrid

Library of Congress Cataloging-in-Publication Data

Bailey, Edward P.
  Writing research papers.

  Bibliography: p.
  Includes index.
  1. Report writing—Handbooks, manuals, etc.
  2. Research—Handbooks, manuals, etc. I. Powell,
  Philip A. II. Title.
  LB1047.3.B34 1986   808'.02   86-19489

ISBN 0-03-006529-1

CBS COLLEGE PUBLISHING
Holt, Rinehart and Winston
The Dryden Press
Saunders College Publishing

Preface

We think our book can be useful to two audiences: those who are writing research papers for academic courses and those who are writing research projects for business purposes.

Although other research books tend to be mainly sources for formats and other conventions (and our book is certainly complete and meets those needs), we've tried to make our book one that can also help people **learn how to go through the research process.**

We suggest a step-by-step approach that many experienced researchers use and that can also be helpful to those who are relatively inexperienced.

We've been careful to illustrate our points throughout with the kind of examples good students might write. We've also tried to write in a clear, personal style not only so readers can understand us but also so the research process will seem less forbidding.

For we believe that the research process is not a forbidding one at all, but instead is a way for all of us to gain access to the wealth of knowledge that has been spoken and written by people of yesterday and today.

We would like to give particular thanks to some real pros—Charlyce Jones Owen, Heidi Anderson, and Sondra Greenfield—our editors at Holt, Rinehart, and Winston. Each made insightful suggestions that became reality in this book. Their active help was invaluable to us, and we want them to know we're very appreciative. We owe them a considerable debt.

Our reviewers were also especially helpful. We appreciate their contributions: Jean Brown, Cedar Valley College; Valerie Davis, Golden West College; Dale S. Huse, Augustana College; David J. Johnson, Edison State College; Marianthe Karanikas, The University of Illinois at Chicago; Muriel Rada, Metropolitan Technical Community College; Robert L. Selig,

Purdue University at Calumet; Thomas F. Shea, Rutgers, The State University of New Jersey.

Finally, our wives—Janet Hiller and Pam Powell—deserve special recognition as our "final" reviewers and daily participants in the revising of this book: reading our drafts, listening to our ideas, suggesting some very key changes. Our special thanks to them.

Contents

1 Introduction to the Research Paper

Have you ever wondered what goes through the minds of newborn infants?

Everything—vague forms all around them, strange shapes, colors, patterns—must be new, and nothing could make much sense.

In fact, do you know that infants don't even know that parts of their bodies belong to them? We learned this striking fact from a quotation in a student's research paper: A baby "lies on his back, kicking his heels and watching the little fists flying past his face. But only very slowly does he learn that they are attached to him and he can control them."[1]

Our point (and the relationship to research papers) is that we all begin life so totally centered within ourselves that we do not understand what is around us, outside us, even at the farther reaches of our own bodies. As we mature, however, we learn more about ourselves and more about our surroundings. The research process—the topic of this book—is one special way of learning what many other people think and have thought, now and down through the ages. It's a way of gaining a new and broader perspective on ourselves, on others, and on our world.

We hope that this book can help you discover the thoughts of others, their experiences, their successes, and their failures. For your research should never—unless you make it so—be dull, dreary, and dusty.

THE STEPS IN WRITING YOUR RESEARCH PAPER

Although you can certainly use this book as a complete reference for documentation, you may also use it as a step-by-step guide to the entire research process. If you're relatively new to research or if you wish to

---

[1] Mary Ann Spencer Pulaski, *Understanding Piaget* (New York: Harper, 1980) 21.

improve your own research process, then you will probably wish to read the chapters in order.

Here's what the book covers:

FINDING A GOOD TOPIC

If you are allowed to choose your own topic, then your first step is to choose a good one, and you really want to find a topic you're interested in. Next, you need to narrow your topic so you can focus it clearly, check to be sure enough research sources are readily available, and then decide whether you want to write an informative or a persuasive paper. Chapter 2, "Finding a Good Topic," will help you find and focus a topic.

FINDING SOURCES FOR YOUR PAPER

Next you want to conduct your research thoroughly. There is a wealth of information available—more than you will ever need or use—on just about any topic. The trick is to find that information easily and quickly. Chapter 3, "Finding Sources for Your Paper," will help you here.

USING YOUR SOURCES

Once you find potential sources, you need to know how to evaluate them and how to keep track of them: what you're sure you will remember today may be (if you're like us) absolutely gone tomorrow. We give you these tips in Chapter 4, "Evaluating Your Sources and Taking Notes."

WRITING YOUR PAPER

The next step (writing your paper) is the key—or, as the Latin phrase says, the *sine qua non* ("without which—nothing").

Chapter 5 covers some fundamentals of writing that are especially important for research papers: the writing process you might wish to use and a discussion of the parts of a standard research paper.

Next you need to know how to use your research material in the paper so that you give proper credit to your sources yet don't end up with a "cut and paste" job (Chapter 6, "Using Sources in Your Paper").

To show you what a final product might look like, in Chapter 7 we give you a very brief (but, we hope, clear and interesting) example of a good research paper.

PREPARING YOUR PAPER IN FINAL FORM

Once you have written a good draft, you'll need to be sure you've followed the conventions most of your readers will expect.

Chapter 8, "The Finished Product: Format Conventions," gives you some detailed rules on such things as how to do an indented quotation, how to quote poetry, how to punctuate with quotation marks, and more.

Chapters 9 and 10 tell you how to document your sources. Chapter 9, "Parenthetical Documentation," gives you a quick overview of the documenting process and some of the general principles you will need to follow. Then Chapter 10, "Works Cited," gives you sample entries to cover almost any situation—from documenting a simple book or article to documenting computer software.

Chapter 11, "Documentation with Notes," tells you how to use a footnote or endnote system in case you do not wish to use the parenthetical system we describe in Chapters 9 and 10.

Chapter 12, "Other Documentation Systems," tells about the APA (American Psychological Association) format and other systems of documentation in case you would like still other alternatives.

TAKING CARE OF SPECIAL SITUATIONS

If you plan to include any illustrations in your paper, you will probably wish to look through Chapter 13, "Illustrations." Illustrations may be troublesome to prepare, but they can be the highlight of a paper.

And if you're writing a paper on a technical subject, you may wish to read Chapter 14, "Special Considerations for the Technical Paper."

These are the steps you'll need to understand. In addition, the Appendix lists some important research aids that can help you find books, articles, and other research material. We've arranged the Appendix by academic discipline (aeronautics, agriculture, and so on) to make it more useful for you, and we've commented briefly on most items.

2

Finding a Good Topic

Sometimes at school—and frequently at work—you can't choose your own research topic: At school, your instructor may ask you to write on something very specific. Or at work, your boss may say, "Find out about such and such and send me a report next week."

In those cases, you just have to do the best you can. But sometimes you have more control over your topic. If so, you should choose your topic very carefully. In fact, the choice of a topic is *crucial* and can often, at this very beginning stage, start you on the road to success—or down that other road.

When you do have the opportunity to choose a topic, then, we suggest you go through the following four steps (the rest of the chapter explains each step in more detail):

- *Choose a topic that interests you.* If you do, you'll find that research can be fun, a positive and enjoyable way to spend your time. If not, imagine the drudgery!

- *Do some preliminary research.* Are there enough research sources available to you? Given plenty of time, especially with the inter-library loan and the computer information systems, you can find just about anything about anything. But few people have the lux-ury of "plenty of time." So before you invest too much time in a topic of your own choosing, you should find out that you can, indeed, turn it into a good research paper—given the resources *you* have available.

- *Narrow your topic.* Some students are skeptical about narrowing a topic, thinking, "If I narrow my topic, don't I just narrow it out of existence, cutting down on the number of sources I can find?" No. Narrowing a topic can *help* you find sources, giving you a sense of direction.

4

• *Decide whether you want to inform your reader what you find in your research or to persuade him or her to believe something.* Both types of paper—informative and persuasive—can be valuable, but knowing your purpose from the beginning can save you time and energy by giving you the right perspective for your research.

FOUR STEPS TO A GOOD RESEARCH TOPIC

Now look more closely at the four steps to finding a good research topic and see how you might go through these steps for two specific topics.

CHOOSING A TOPIC THAT INTERESTS YOU

Of course there's no single way to choose a topic, but *all* people who are alive have interests. Have you ever been intrigued while browsing through encyclopedias? (Topics like *diamonds, the Alamo, poison ivy,* or the explorer *La Salle* might catch your eye.) Or while looking randomly on the shelves of the library? Or while talking to new acquaintances about places you have never been and things you have never done? Most of us have had those experiences. These are some ways you can find interesting topics.

If you have a truly blank check for a topic (you can write on anything you wish), you might try some of these methods—browsing, looking randomly, talking—as ways to stimulate your imagination and to generate interesting topics. They are guaranteed to work.

But if you don't have a blank check—just a general topic you're expected to deal with—you should still work to make your final topic something interesting. Try to find a way to slant the topic to *your* interests.

For example, suppose you are assigned to write about American architecture in the early 1900s. In general, that topic may not interest you. But you may be interested in finding out more about the skyscrapers in New York . . . or the limited building materials the architects had to deal with then . . . or even that funny little church around the corner. Allow yourself to be creative and you will find that special slant that will make you feel, "Now *that's* something interesting!"

DOING PRELIMINARY RESEARCH

Before you get really involved with a potential topic, you need to find out quickly if it will work for you—in your situation, with your time limit, and with your resources.

To find out more about your topic, go to the easiest sources you can find. The encyclopedia comes quickly to mind for many topics. Read an article in the encyclopedia about your topic. Then turn to other articles—related to your topic—in the same encyclopedia. Next look through another encyclopedia (the treatments of subjects can be surprisingly different). Each time, be sure to look for a list of additional references at the ends of the articles (some encyclopedias have these lists). These references can be good leads to research sources later on.

Then check the card catalog for some books on your topic and perhaps ask the reference librarian if he or she thinks your library can support your topic easily. After only half an hour or so, you should have learned much more about your topic and about the research material available for it.

If the encyclopedia doesn't cover your topic—perhaps your topic is too recent?—then try some other sources that come to mind easily: a newspaper, a friend who knows something about it, a professor who knows about it or knows someone who does, or the reference librarian. There is almost always a quick way to get some preliminary information about almost anything. Our next chapter tells you more about how to find sources, but you probably will not even need to consult it to find the kind of quick, general information you want at this stage.

If you're uneasy about your topic or the resources available after your preliminary research (and if you have the option), you need to think about changing the topic: Perhaps your preliminary research triggered a different slant on your topic or perhaps you will need to change your topic entirely.

If you do feel that your topic is questionable, you need to take corrective steps right away. All too often, people who wait become trapped by a bad topic and are destined for trouble.

NARROWING YOUR TOPIC

As your research progresses—and before you actually begin writing the paper—you will want to be able to state your topic in a single sentence, which we'll call a **thesis sentence.** Here are some thesis sentences that would probably work well for most research papers:

> Let me tell you how diamonds are mined.
>
> The decision of the Texans to defend the Alamo was foolhardy.
>
> The parochialism of the early modern Olympics caused international bitterness.

The first topic, *let me tell you how diamonds are mined,* is simply informative; the other two are persuasive. We'll go into more detail in the next section on how to decide which type of paper to write—informative or persuasive. For now, though, you just have to be aware that the two different types exist.

- *Begin with the noun.* Most topics start as very general nouns: "diamonds," "the Alamo," "the Olympics." Your first step in narrowing is to make that noun more specific. Let's illustrate with the general topic of "diamonds." Here are a few ways to make that general topic more specific:

finding diamonds in the earth

cutting diamonds to give them their sparkle

wholesaling diamonds

the political laws that protect the mining of diamonds

the health problems of those who mine diamonds

the procedure for mining diamonds

See how many different directions—different "slants"—you can take for the topic of "diamonds"? The same possibilities exist for almost every general subject. And remember that even a narrowed topic that may sound rather dull—"the wholesaling of diamonds," for example—can be fascinating. Do you know that one family controls the sale of diamonds throughout the world? How did that family get that control? And how does it keep it? So don't be too quick to discard narrowed topics.

Producing a thesis sentence for informative papers

If you're writing an informative paper, you're now ready to write your thesis sentence—one sentence that states the narrowed subject of your research paper. Simply write "Let me tell you about . . ." and then add your narrowed topic:

Let me tell you about the health problems of those who mine diamonds.

Let me tell you about how the De Beers family gained control of the diamond market.

Let me tell you about how diamonds are mined.

Of course, you will probably change the wording of this thesis sentence once you actually write your paper. Some instructors, in fact, will ask you not to use the first person ("I") in your thesis statement. Now, however, it serves as a constant guide to you as you conduct your research.

Producing a thesis sentence for persuasive papers

If you are writing a persuasive paper, you must, of course, express an opinion about your topic. So to produce a thesis sentence you must take your narrowed topic and add your opinion to it. Here are two sample opinions you could add to the narrowed topic of "the mining of diamonds":

> The mining of diamonds is hazardous to the health of the miners.

> The mining of diamonds is bringing a better economy to the impoverished workers.

A good opinion, by the way, doesn't have to be an unusual one. Most of the time, your reader won't have any preconceived opinion about your topic and will be open to what you say as long as you do not seem ridiculous ("the mining of diamonds is simple and fun for the miners" would probably be ridiculous).

A good opinion, therefore, should seem reasonable. It should also be fairly precise. For example, "the mining of diamonds is bad" is obviously so imprecise that it's ambiguous for the reader (in fact, it probably was ambiguous for the writer).

Finally, a good opinion should be something you believe in. Instead of saying that "Mining diamonds should be outlawed because of health hazards," which may seem rather extreme to you, you might say this: "*Some techniques* for mining diamonds should be outlawed because of health hazards."

A summary of the process for narrowing a topic

To begin narrowing a topic, then, start with the noun ("diamonds") and then add words to make that noun more specific ("the mining of diamonds").

If you plan to write an *informative* paper, simply begin your new narrowed topic with "Let me tell you about . . .": "*Let me tell you about how diamonds are mined.*"

If you plan to write a *persuasive* paper, simply add your opinion to the new narrowed topic: "The mining of diamonds *is hazardous to the health of the miners.*"

By the way, this is not a process that you can always (or even usually) complete while doing your preliminary research. You need to start narrowing as soon as you can, and, as you learn more about your topic, you need to stay alert for better ways to narrow it and (for a persuasive paper) better ways to express your opinion. You'll probably be fine-tuning, adjusting, and fiddling with the thesis sentence frequently. But the sooner you can get a fairly good thesis sentence, the better you'll be able to do your research *and* your writing later.

DECIDING WHICH TYPE OF RESEARCH PAPER TO WRITE

Now look more closely at the types of paper you can write. Almost all research papers, in college or outside of it, are either **informative** or **persuasive.**

If you decide to write an *informative paper,* you'll simply tell the reader some interesting things you have discovered. To continue with our example, you might tell how diamonds are mined in Africa. You won't pass judgment on the efficiency of the mining process or on its fairness or unfairness to the miners. You'll simply tell (or "inform") your reader about what happens.

If you decide to write a *persuasive paper,* however, you *will* pass judgment. You will go beyond informing and try to convince your reader to believe something: perhaps (though unlikely) that "mining diamonds is a model process other industries should follow" or that "mining diamonds creates devastating health problems for the workers," or whatever your point may be.

What type of paper should you write if you have a choice: informative or persuasive?

The pros and cons of informative papers

Informing is almost always easier than persuading and is still a very worthwhile way to learn most of the fundamentals of research. An advantage—especially if you have a "blank check" for choosing a topic—is that you will have a wealth of topics to choose from: There are many, many fascinating things that would be interesting for you (and your reader) to learn more about.

There is one occasional drawback for informative papers, though. If you are writing about something you know little about, you may find one good source that says it all, says it in the right amount of detail, and says it better than you think you can. Then what? You may find you have little of your own to say, wishing you could just reproduce that good source and hand it in.

On the other hand, not all topics have that one good source. Sometimes, you can find out enough about a topic so that you can write about it for your audience better than the authors of any of your individual sources wrote to their audiences.

The drawback, then, for an informative paper is not necessarily disabling: Probably most good research is more informative than it is persuasive.

The pros and cons of persuasive papers

Persuasive papers are often a little harder to write than informative ones, but you will probably have less trouble being tied to one good source. For in writing a persuasive paper you will probably want to concentrate more on *your* ideas, *your* opinions, *your* logic. You will simply use somebody else's facts (and some of their ideas, opinions, and logic) as supporting material embedded in your thinking.

What are the difficulties of writing persuasive papers? Too often students have trouble finding enough solid research material to come up with persuasive points they really believe, deep in their hearts. Is diamond mining really devastating to the miners' health? Too often students aren't really sure, but to meet the assignment, they feel forced to choose a side and defend it as an academic exercise.

Should you write an informative or a persuasive paper? There are built-in appeals and difficulties for both. And both, done well, can be valuable for both the writer and the reader. If you discover, through your research, that you have developed a strong belief, then write a persuasive paper. But if you have not developed such a belief, then we recommend that you not try to pretend you have developed one. The pretense will be difficult for you to maintain and may be noticeable to the reader.

Now let us look, briefly, at how you might go through the steps for writing a research paper that we have discussed so far.

TENTATIVE TOPIC: "THE BATTLE OF THE ALAMO"

Suppose you can choose any topic you wish for your research paper. First, go to the encyclopedias and begin browsing.

You begin with the letter "A" and soon run across "Alamo." As you browse through the article, you discover that there is some question about why the Texans remained at the fort to fight. According to the encyclopedia, "Gen. Sam Houston ordered the Alamo abandoned and destroyed. Instead, the garrison chose to defend it."[1] Was the garrison's insubordination (not abandoning the fort when ordered to do so) based on something Houston did not know or care about? Was the garrison's decision a wise one that simply backfired, killing them? Perhaps it was a brave decision in the face of almost certain annihilation, designed to rally the other Texans to the cause? Or was it simply foolish bravado?

At this point, you think you have not only a topic, but maybe even a narrowed topic: "The decision of the Texans to defend the Alamo." You think you would like to write a persuasive paper asserting the decision

---

[1] "Alamo." *Encyclopedia Americana.* 1983 ed.

was wise or foolhardy, but right now you don't know enough to take a stand. So you decide to look further.

You notice that there is a list of references at the end of the article in the encyclopedia, so you jot down the items on the list for further reading. One of the items is a book called *A Time to Stand.* You find it in the library's card catalog; record the call number, title, and author; and locate the book on the library shelves. Next to that book are two others, *The Alamo* and *13 Days to Glory.*

When you look through the books, you are disappointed. For the most part, the tone of all three books calls their credibility into question: They seem bent more on glorifying the Texans than in dispassionately presenting history. Worse, there is significant disagreement even on the basic facts of what happened at the Alamo: Did Sam Houston (who was not at the Alamo himself) really send an order for the Texans to abandon the Alamo? Or did Sam Houston, instead, send a representative, Jim Bowie, to look things over first? What did happen?

The encyclopedia, which had gotten you started on this topic in the first place, had not raised any such questions. It had stated clearly that Sam Houston had given the order. The book you have just found, *A Time to Stand,* seems to agree: "Actually, the evidence indicates that Houston did indeed try to avert the siege by ordering the Alamo destroyed and the garrison withdrawn."[2]

Your next book, *The Alamo,* disagrees with the one you have just looked at, saying Houston did *not* give an order but simply sent Jim Bowie as his representative: "Houston sent a valued counselor with a detachment of reinforcements. . . . On that man's shoulders rested the responsibility of advising as to whether or not Bexar [the location of the Alamo] should be evacuated and the Alamo blown up."[3]

You're worried that if you can't even get the facts straight, you may have difficulty deciding whether the Texans made a wise or a foolish decision to remain and fight. You hope that other sources may prove more helpful, so you look for lists of references at the ends of the three books you have. All three—*A Time to Stand, The Alamo,* and *13 Days to Glory*—have lengthy lists. Unfortunately, many of the items are ancient newspapers, obscure documents, personal interviews, books that might be out of print or unavailable, and locally published pamphlets.

Even worse, you find this evaluation of sources in the bibliography section of *13 Days to Glory:*

> For all this, it must be admitted that the historical material about the Al-
> amo is disappointingly slight. As James Atkins Shackford observes in his
> *Davy Crockett* (1956): "I suppose no event in recent historical times, with a

[2] Walter Lord, *A Time to Stand* (New York: Harper, 1961) 200.
[3] John Myers Myers, *The Alamo* (New York: Dutton, 1948) 88.

basis in fact, has been more conducive to the creation of legend, fiction, gossip, error and falsehood than the destruction of the fortress at San Antonio de Bexar. . . . Except for the date and the fact of its fall, there is almost no single point about the Alamo upon which testimony of the few survivors does not disagree."[4]

Now you are really worried. You have found a topic that might be challenging to a professional historian. You have not looked for articles yet, you have not checked the card catalog fully, but you are skeptical that your library—or *any* library—can support your topic.

What should you do? You could continue with the idea of writing a persuasive paper. Some of the sources in the backs of those three books might be available. There might be something really good right in your library. But if you have the choice of any topic, and if you are not especially intrigued with this topic, you could consider these two other options:

- Write on something entirely different.
- Change the slant of your paper.

Your best bet might, surprisingly, be the second option: Change the slant of your paper. You could convert your weakness to a strength by writing about the *lack* of good information about the Alamo. How about this for a thesis sentence: "There are many controversial questions about even the basic facts of what happened at the Alamo"? Now you can write a persuasive paper convincing your reader that there is a lot of controversy.

You could even change the slant so much that you write an *informative* paper: "Let me tell you about some of the controversies surrounding the Battle of the Alamo."

Or you could choose the first option above and write on something entirely different. But you might be missing a good bet.

TENTATIVE TOPIC: "THE OLYMPICS"

Suppose you're interested in the Olympic Games. There's something especially significant—and different—about them, and no athletic prize has seemed more valued than an Olympic gold medal. You don't have any particular aspect of the Olympics that interests you at this point, so you decide to browse through the encyclopedias.

The *Encyclopaedia Britannica* in your library has a good article on the Olympics, including charts of winners. As you read, you think the ancient

---

[4] Lon Tinkle, *13 Days to Glory: The Siege of the Alamo* (New York: McGraw, 1958) 248. Ellipsis is in the original.

games could be the basis for a good paper, but then you become intrigued by the following paragraph about the early "revived" games—those starting about a century ago:

> It was through the efforts of Baron Pierre de Coubertin (1863–1937) of France, a brilliant educator and scholar but not an athlete, that the Olympic Games were revived. Having decided that at least one of the reasons for the glory of the Golden Age of Greece was the emphasis placed on physical culture and frequent athletic festivals, he concluded that nothing but good could result if the athletes of all countries of the world were brought together once every four years on the friendly fields of amateur sport, unmindful of national rivalries, jealousies, and differences of all kinds and with all considerations of politics, race, religion, wealth, and social status eliminated.[5]

You're struck by the irony that the recent games have hardly met the Baron's ideal. The Olympics you can remember have been filled with political controversy and even bloodshed. Perhaps you could write a persuasive paper showing that the Olympics led to international divisiveness instead of international unity. That would make your paper persuasive. You now have a somewhat narrowed topic for your thesis sentence, "the modern Olympics," and an opinion, "divisive."

You need to learn more about your topic to see whether it is as workable as it seems at this point. In the card catalog you find five books that have potential. When you go to the shelves, you find in one of them, *The Story of the Olympic Games* by John Kieran and Arthur Daley, that even the early "revived" Olympics were controversial. That is something of a surprise since you're familiar with only the problems in the more recent games. You know you can't write about controversies in each of the modern Olympic games—there would be too many details to cover adequately—and you think most people would be as surprised as you were, and as interested, in the controversies in the games around 1900. So you decide to focus on those early games. You will keep the opinion "divisive" but narrow your topic even further from "the modern Olympics" to "the *early* modern Olympics." You now have your working thesis sentence: "The early modern Olympics were divisive."

So you have now gone through the four steps we recommended in this chapter:

1. Choosing a topic that interests you: the Olympics.
2. Doing some quick, preliminary research in an encyclopedia and in some books that were easy to find.

---

[5] "Olympic Games," *Encyclopaedia Britannica,* 1973 ed.

3. Narrowing your topic from "the Olympics" to "the *early modern* Olympics" and adding an opinion to it.
4. Deciding to write a *persuasive* paper instead of an informative one.

You now should be at least fairly confident that you have a good topic, one you can find sources on easily. You know you will have to start looking through more and different sources (the newspapers from the turn of the century might be useful and fun). As you look further, you may need to adjust your thesis sentence some more. But you're off to a good start.

By the way, the sample research paper in this book is called "Controversy in the Early Modern Olympics," and it grew out of the research we just recounted. You may wish to turn to Chapter 7 now and read that sample paper.

POSSIBLE TOPICS

What do most teachers consider the most clichéd topic of modern times? If you said "capital punishment," you guessed right.

But the *topic* isn't really the problem: The problem is how the writer deals with the topic. For example, George Orwell has written an absolutely superb essay on capital punishment called "A Hanging." Now that esssay is not a traditional research paper, but it is certainly a persuasive paper on what many would consider to be a trite tcpic. The result, however, is anything but trite. So remember that the way you handle the topic is more important than the topic itself.

Here are some possible topics to help get you going (they will of course need considerable narrowing):

alcoholism	new technical developments
antiburglary devices	nuclear energy
ballet	photography
beach preservation	planets
chemical fertilizers	poisons
child custody	prisons
computers	pyramids
country music	pythons
diets	Quakers
drug addiction	quilting bees in the 1800s
economy of United States	railroads
endangered animals	rain forests
fantasy fiction	rehabilitation of prisoners
farm life in the Middle Ages	religious celebrations
food preservation	reflecting telescopes
French cooking	road construction

fungicides
gambling
health foods
incurable diseases
insulation
Islamic movements
knee operations
lighthouses
marathons
mass transportation
midwives
Native Americans

sharks
social problems today
space exploration
speech disorders
spiders that kill
strip-mining
tax reform
treason
Vikings
water sources
wilderness preservation
yoga

EXERCISES

A. Choose any five general topics from pages 14–15 and narrow each one to a thesis sentence suitable for an *informative* paper.

Example:
General Topic: lighthouses
Thesis Sentence: Let me tell you about the roles nineteenth-century American lighthouses played as navigational aids for ships.

1. General Topic:_____

   Thesis Sentence:_____

   _____

2. General Topic:_____

   Thesis Sentence:_____

   _____

3. General Topic:_____

   Thesis Sentence:_____

   _____

4. General Topic:_____

   Thesis Sentence:_____

   _____

5. General Topic:_____

   Thesis Sentence:_____

   _____

B. Choose the same general topics you used for Exercise A and turn each one into a thesis sentence suitable for a *persuasive* paper (add your opinion to the narrowed topic).

Example:
General Topic: lighthouses
Thesis Sentence: Nineteenth-century American lighthouses were not very effective as navigational aids for ships.

1. General Topic:_____

   Thesis Sentence:_____

   _____

2. General Topic:_____

   Thesis Sentence:_____

   _____

3. General Topic:_____

   Thesis Sentence:_____

   _____

4. General Topic:_____

   Thesis Sentence:_____

   _____

5. General Topic:_____

   Thesis Sentence:_____

   _____

C. Choose an interesting topic for a research paper that would be about 5 to 10 pages long (or a length your instructor assigns). Then do some quick preliminary research, finding at least one source to confirm that your topic seems workable (if it's not, choose another topic). Then narrow your topic and write a tentative thesis sentence for either an informative or a persuasive paper.

Proposed General Topic:_____

Preliminary Source (Author, Title, Date, Pages):_____

_____

_____

Thesis Sentence (Informative or Persuasive):_____

_____

_____

3

Finding Sources
for Your Paper

This chapter and the next cover the fundamentals of the research process. Basically, the research process we recommend is this:

- Go to the card catalog in the library and list all the books you think might have good material for your topic. Then find those books, evaluate them, and take notes on the ones that do, in fact, have good material.
- Also go to the various bibliographies and indexes for magazines and newspapers to identify the articles you think might be helpful. Then find, evaluate, and take notes on those articles.
- Also, consider alternative sources—such as interviews, movies, or videotapes—that could be the highlight of your paper.
- And meanwhile, have a tentative—or working—outline that you are developing, expanding, and refining as you gather more and more information about your topic.

For convenience, we've divided the research process into two parts, even though you will actually work back and forth between them. This chapter tells you how to find books and articles. The next chapter tells you how to evaluate those sources, take notes from them, and develop a working outline for your paper.

Before delving in, we should clear up a point that sometimes is confusing. The traditional research process involves keeping track of *two* kinds of information: *Bibliography cards* list the title, author, and other such identifying information about possible sources; *note cards,* on the other hand, list quotations, paraphrases, and summaries of information you've found in those sources.

We suggest you use two different sizes of cards just to keep them from getting mixed up: smaller 3 × 5 cards for the bibliography cards, and larger 4 × 6 or 5 × 8 cards for the note cards (which may well contain more information). For people who find making bibliography and note cards more work than they are worth, we will suggest alternatives in the next chapter.

For this chapter we will talk about *identifying* sources and keeping track of them on *bibliography cards.*

Finally, you may be wondering about computers. Have libraries joined the computer generation? Absolutely. There are some exciting innovations that we will also discuss in this chapter.

THE LIBRARY

The key to most research is the library. Occasionally, you'll be able to use personal interviews or questionnaires as research material. In fact, we *highly* recommend you try these methods—especially the interview (there is almost always someone available who would have some interesting and insightful things to say about most topics). Yet the library is frequently the starting point for research, so we'll begin there.

You're already familiar with the circulation desk where you check out books and with the card catalog (though we'll cover this in more detail in a minute). And you may not have had much occasion to use other parts of the library such as the audiovisual section or the rare-books section. So we'll cover those sections of the library that are especially important to you now as you prepare to write a research paper.

REFERENCE SECTION

Suddenly the reference section is one of the most important places in the library. It gathers conveniently in one place most of the books you'll need to help you find material in the rest of the library. It has *indexes* and *bibliographies,* which list books and articles in books, magazines, and newspapers; and it has *abstracts,* which briefly summarize some of the articles in those sources. We'll cover indexes, bibliographies, and abstracts in detail in this chapter. A reference section also has encyclopedias, collections of biographies, atlases, almanacs, and other very basic sources of information.

You can't check out most material in the reference section because it has to be available all the time to everyone who needs it. This may seem a disadvantage since you have to use the material in the library, but it's actually a big advantage to you because the reference material always should be there for you to use.

RESERVE SECTION

College and university libraries often have a reserve section that contains books and other material you can check out for only a short time—perhaps for as little as an hour or perhaps overnight. Some books and articles are used so frequently that they need to be available to a large number of people on short notice. However, since these materials change often, depending on the courses being taught, they aren't kept in the reference section.

PERIODICAL SECTION

A periodical is, loosely, a magazine or a newspaper—something printed regularly (or periodically), such as daily, weekly, or quarterly. *Newsweek,* for example, is a periodical. More scholarly magazines, such as *American Psychologist, Comparative Political Studies, Journal of Renaissance and Baroque Music,* and *Nineteenth Century Fiction,* are special types of periodicals called "journals."

There are three important parts to the periodical section:

List of periodicals

Usually a library has a list of all the periodicals available there. It could be a short list posted on a wall. Often, though, it is a large computer listing lying conspicuously on a table in the area near the periodical shelves. When you compile the bibliography cards for your paper, you'll no doubt end up with many magazines and journal articles you'll want to read. The list of periodicals will tell you if the publications are available in your library.

Current issues

The current issues, usually all those for the current year, often are displayed in one part of the periodical section.

Back issues

When issues are no longer current, they're usually collected by volume or year, bound with a hard cover (like a book), and placed in the "back issues" part of the periodical section. Some back issues also may be on microfilm (a roll of film) or microfiche (a card of film).

MICROFILM AND MICROFICHE SECTION

The microfilm/microfiche—or microform—section sometimes intimidates people because they have to learn to operate special pieces of equipment to read the microform material, which contains books, magazines, and newspapers filmed in very reduced size. Actually microform readers are easy to use, and some allow you to print pages (for a small price). The microform section contains such items as back issues of *The New York Times* and *Times* of London, back issues of some periodicals, and rare books. *The New York Times* is an extremely valuable source, so we'll talk about it later in the chapter.

FINDING BOOKS

Once you have a good topic, your first task in the library is to compile a working bibliography—a list of books and articles that might be useful.

Where should you start? Although articles are often more up-to-date, we suggest you start with books. Why? Three reasons: Books are often easier to find than articles; they're more likely to have a list of other sources we might want to find; and they usually cover topics more generally than articles do.

This last point is important: A book is often perfectly willing to give the standard, accepted view on any topic; an article, on the other hand, usually takes issue with the standard view. Want to find the standard interpretation of a Faulkner novel? Go to a book that deals with many of the novels and you will have at least a fairly good chance of getting the commonly accepted interpretation. But why would somebody write an article giving the already accepted interpretation?

What this all boils down to is this: You're often better off looking for information in books first; then go to articles for more specialized information.

THE CARD CATALOG

The key to finding books is the card catalog—in one form or another.

Today, many libraries have the "card catalog" on a computer. You simply ask the computer for what you need and it responds. In a way, that's a great advance: You can get the information quickly, painlessly, and in one central location. On the other hand, by using a computer you miss all those titles you just happened to notice while thumbing through the card catalog. And, often, those chance sightings can prove to be very important in your research.

So right now, card catalogs exist in the traditional form (a large file of 3 × 5 cards in alphabetical order) and a computerized form. In this book, we'll concentrate on the traditional card catalog for two reasons: First, many traditional card catalogs still exist; second, by understanding the workings of the traditional card catalog, you will have no trouble adjusting almost instantly to whichever of the various computer systems your library may have. Right now, the traditional card catalog is fairly

Author card

```
PS        Longley, John Lewis.
3511          The tragic mask; a study of Faulkner's heroes.
.A86      Chapel Hill, University of North Carolina Press
Z88       [1963]

              242 p.  24 cm.


              1. Faulkner, William, 1897–1962. 2. Heroes in
          literature. I. Title.
          PS3511.A86Z88          813.52          63-22806

          Library of Congress          [5]
```

Title card

```
          The tragic mask

PS        Longley, John Lewis.
3511          The tragic mask; a study of Faulkner's heroes.
.A86      Chapel Hill, University of North Carolina Press
Z88       [1963]

              242 p.  24 cm.


              1. Faulkner, William, 1897–1962. 2. Heroes in
          literature. I. Title.
          PS3511.A86Z88          813.52          63-22806

          Library of Congress          [5]
```

Subject card

```
          FAULKNER, WILLIAM, 1897-1962

PS        Longley, John Lewis.
3511          The tragic mask; a study of Faulkner's heroes.
.A86      Chapel Hill, University of North Carolina Press
Z88       [1963]

              242 p.  24 cm.


              1. Faulkner, William, 1897–1962. 2. Heroes in
          literature. I. Title.
          PS3511.A86Z88          813.52          63-22806

          Library of Congress          [5]
```

standard; but standards are still developing for the computerized system.

In a traditional card catalog system, then, there are at least *three* cards for each book: an *author card,* filed alphabetically by the author's last name; a *title card,* filed alphabetically by the title of the book; and at least one *subject card,* filed alphabetically by the subject of the book. Three sample cards for a book by John Longley called *The Tragic Mask* are on the facing page.

All three of these cards start as author cards. The difference is that a title card has the title typed on top so it can be alphabetized by the title more easily, and the subject card has the subject typed on top so it can be alphabetized by subject.

Sometimes all three kinds of card are in the same catalog, and sometimes they're filed separately. For example, you might find one card catalog for author and title cards and another card catalog for subject cards.

When you're beginning your research, you probably won't know any authors or titles, so you will first look under the subject you're interested in. Let's look more closely at a subject card to see what information is particularly helpful:

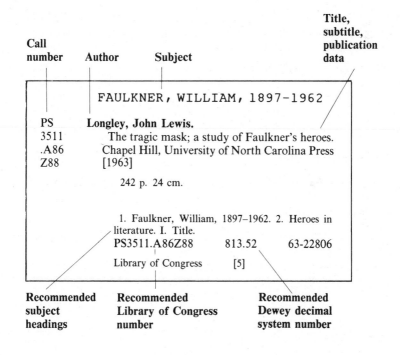

CLASSIFICATION SYSTEMS

Libraries arrange their books by either the Dewey decimal classification system or, even more popular for large libraries, the Library of Congress classification system. You don't need to memorize these systems, but you'll have an easier time finding the books on the shelves if you understand how these systems work.

Dewey Decimal System

This system uses primarily numbers rather than letters and numbers, and it divides all knowledge into major categories:

000   General Works
100   Philosophy and Related Disciplines
200   Religion
300   Social Sciences
400   Language
500   Pure Science
600   Applied Science
700   Arts
800   Literature
900   General Geography, History, Travel, and Collected Biography
  B   Individual Biographies
  F   Fiction in English

These numbers then become more and more specific until they identify a book. For example, 800 (Literature) can be narrowed to 810 (American Literature) to 813 (Fiction in American Literature) and so on to 813.52, which is John Longley's *The Tragic Mask* (the book listed on the sample card we just showed you). The library where we found that card doesn't use the Dewey Decimal System, but a suggested Dewey Decimal System number is on the bottom of the card to help those libraries that do use it.

Library of Congress System

Our sample card on *The Tragic Mask* does use the Library of Congress System, which uses letter and numbers. Again, all knowledge first is classified into broad categories:

A   General Works
B   Philosophy, Psychology, Religion
C–D   History and Topology (except America)
E–F   History and Topology: America
G   Geography and Anthropology
H   Social Sciences
J   Political Science
K   Law
L   Education
M   Music
N   Fine Arts
P   Language and Literature
Q   Science
R   Medicine
S   Agriculture and Forestry
T   Technology

U   Military Science
V   Naval Science
Z   Bibliography

By adding another letter (*PS*, for example, means American Literature) and numbers, we can finally identify a specific book. Thus, PS/3511/.A86/ Z88 identifies Longley's *The Tragic Mask*.

BIBLIOGRAPHY CARDS FOR BOOKS

Now that you know how the card catalog is arranged and basically how books are classified, what should you do to find books for your paper? Start by going to the appropriate subject heading in the card catalog. Look for books that might be helpful, and also look for other possible subject headings near the bottoms of the cards in that section of the card catalog.

If you know very little about your subject, you may want to identify one or two books, find them on the shelves, and look them over to be sure your topic is sound or to help narrow it even more.

As you identify books—whether one or two for preliminary reading or a comprehensive list of what's available in your library—jot down key information on your 3 × 5 bibliography cards. Don't waste time by listing publication data now since many of the books you identify from the card catalog may not end up being helpful. For now, just list enough information so you can find the book on the shelves—the call number, author, and title. Here's a sample:

PS
3511
.A86
Z88

Longley, John Lewis
The Tragic Mask

Once you actually have the book in your hands and decide that it will be useful to you, then take the information from the book itself to complete your working bibliography card. You'll need all of the following items later (the ones that are applicable) when you are preparing your parenthetical references and Works Cited section:

author(s) or group responsible
title and subtitle (and volume title if part of a multivolume set)
translator(s)
editor(s)
edition (don't worry about number of "printings," but do note the edition if the book is other than the first edition)
series (such as "Studies in Linguistics, No. 3")
volume numbers(s)
place of publication (the first one listed if there are several, unless you have some reason for showing a different one)
publisher
date of publication (latest copyright date, not the date of printing)

Don't worry at this point about the right format if you don't know it. You can worry about that when you are putting your paper in final form. (Chapters 9 and 10 give formats for parenthetical references and Works Cited, while Chapters 11 and 12 cover other documentation styles; all the documentation styles use some form of bibliographic entry, similar to those illustrated in Chapter 10.) Of course, you can save yourself some time by recording the information in the form you'll need later for the Works Cited entries.

Here's what our sample working bibliography card looks like after we've found the book and decided that it's useful:

PS
3511
.A86
Z88

LO

Longley, John Lewis
The Tragic Mask : A Study of Faulkner's Heroes

Chapel Hill, N.C.
University of North
Carolina Press
1963

good detail

Notice that we've added two letters in the upper right corner of the card. These two letters are a code for the book—we use the first two letters of the author's last name. This code will be valuable later when we're taking notes from the book. Then we'll use these code letters on the note cards to identify the source of the material rather than writing down more complete bibliographic information on each note card. By the way, if an author has written more than one book that we're using, we use the first two letters of the last name and then the first letter from a main word in the title: "LO/T." We'll illustrate this system further in Chapter 4.

We've added a comment on the bottom of our working bibliography card: "good detail." That's a reminder for later that the source seemed to have particularly useful information. You should annotate all your working bibliography cards once you've found the source—or even if you haven't. Such annotations as "not on the shelves" and "particularly good on *As I Lay Dying*" can be valuable later.

ESSAY AND GENERAL LITERATURE INDEX

You know that the card catalog is the key to finding books on your topic. But how do you find just parts of books—essays in them or chapters—when the book itself is on something more general?

The *Essay and General Literature Index* can help: It has been published since 1900 and indexes, each year, about 4,000 essays in about 300 different books—not very comprehensive considering the number of books in a library that contain essays, but perhaps helpful and well worth checking for general topics or topics on literature. Here's just part of an entry in the 1983 volume on William Faulkner:

The sound and the fury

Bleikasten, A. Bloom and Quentin. *In* The Seventh of Joyce, ed. by B. Benstock p100-08

Pitavy, F. L. Idiocy and idealism: a reflection on the Faulknerian idiot. *In* Faulkner and idealism, ed. by M. Gresset and P. Samway p97-111

Pitavy, F. L. Joyce's and Faulkner's "twining stresses": a textual comparison. *In* The Seventh of Joyce, ed. by B. Benstock p90-99

Walker, N. Stephen and Quentin. *In* The Seventh of Joyce, ed. by B. Benstock p109-13

The wild palms

Meindl, D. Romantic idealism and The wild palms. *In* Faulkner and idealism, ed. by M. Gresset and P. Samway p86-96

Bibliography

Zender, K. F. Faulkner. *In* American literary scholarship, 1981 p145-70

How do you read those entries? The first, by A. Bleikasten, is called "Bloom and Quentin." It's on pages 100–108 of a book called *The Seventh of Joyce,* edited by B. Benstock.

But notice the last entry in the excerpt: a 25-page *bibliography* (a list of books and articles about Faulkner). That bibliography could well be your best find—one of the most important items you'll discover in all of your research. Always keep alert for such bibliographies. If you find one for your topic, you'll greatly simplify your research by "piggy-backing" on the work someone else has already done! In research as in other matters, there's no need to reinvent the wheel.

Once you've made a list of books from the card catalog and, if applicable, from the *Essay and General Literature Index,* you probably should go to those books before looking further for sources. What you find in those books may alter your topic enough to change the periodical articles you'll be interested in. Chapter 4 tells you what to do once you've found a potentially helpful source and are ready to take notes.

For now, though, let's go directly to periodicals and *their* various "card catalogs."

FINDING PERIODICALS

There isn't a single card catalog for periodicals. You can't go one place, pull out a few file trays, and find everything you need. But there are a number of reference books with organized lists of articles in periodicals (and sometimes selected books, too). These reference books serve as "miniature card catalogs" for such academic fields as biology, general science, and so forth. There are many such books available, but not specific ones for all disciplines, so you may have to be something of a detective.

When you find a reference book that appears useful, take a few minutes to see what publications it covers, how it arranges information, and what abbreviations and symbols it uses. Finding out the publications covered will help you judge the usefulness of the reference book itself. Seeing how the information is arranged will help you decide what subject you want to look for first and may help you think of related topics to check on. And the list of abbreviations and symbols probably will be necessary to understand the items you find, since most reference books rely heavily on abbreviations and symbols to save space.

INDEXES

An index usually doesn't tell how valuable a source is, or even exactly what it's about (titles can be misleading), but at least it tells you something exists. It's like a single, well-organized table of contents (arranged by subject) for all the periodicals it indexes. Some indexes list a few selected books, but for the most part they're limited to articles in periodicals. You might have to check several volumes of an index, depending on how many years you're interested in, but using an index is easier than wandering aimlessly through shelf after shelf of periodicals. Your challenge, then, is to find the right indexes for your topic.

There are literally hundreds of indexes. We can't cover all of them in this book, but we can look here at the most common ones, the ones that can serve as starting points for most research paper topics. In addition, the Appendix at the back of this book lists some other indexes under their academic subjects.

Readers' Guide to Periodical Literature

This is the most widely known of the indexes. It covers about 200 popular or general-interest magazines and journals: *Time, U.S. News & World Report, Reader's Digest, Popular Mechanics, Scientific American, Sky and Telescope*, and so forth. Essentially, then, this index—like all of the other indexes—is a collected "table of contents" for all those magazines it covers.

But unlike the table of contents for a book or a magazine (which is organized by page number—the order articles or chapters appear), this "table of contents" is organized by subject. Under a heading such as "Guided Missiles," then, you will find a list of *all* the articles from *all* the magazines (published during a twelve-month period) indexed by *Readers' Guide*.

Because *Readers' Guide* indexes mainly popular magazines and journals, it may not help much for a scholarly topic—one on literary criticism, for example.

If you're interested in writing about William Faulkner, you would probably be making a mistake consulting the *Readers' Guide*. Other indexes, such as an index published by the Modern Language Association (which we'll discuss shortly), would be much better. But for a topic like "Mental Depression," you would get over forty entries in the March 1984–February 1985 issue. Here's a sample so you can see what entries look like:

> **Depression, Mental**
> *See also*
> Seasonal affective disorder
> The agony of depression [with editorial comment by Kevin Doyle] J. O'Hara. il *Macleans* 97:2, 46-52 Mr 19 '84
> Are you happy? Don't feel guilty about sometimes being depressed; you have the right to be unhappy. L. Hazleton. il *Glamour* 82:123 O '84
> Childhood depression. J. Costello. il *Parents* 58:117 D '83

The first entry is a seven-page, illustrated article in *Macleans* called "The Agony of Depression." The key at the front of issue of *Readers' Guide* helps you decode the symbols.

The entry we just showed you, as we said, comes from the March 1984–February 1985 issue. Since that issue covers only the articles that were published during that twelve-month period, you might want to consult earlier and later issues. The *earlier* issues are generally collected similarly into twelve-month cumulations. The *later, contemporary* issues come out every two weeks until there are enough for the next twelve-month cumulation. Most other indexes are published similarly.

PAIS Bulletin

If you're writing on a popular topic, you might get even more help from the *Public Affairs Information Service Bulletin*. Like *Readers' Guide*, *PAIS* indexes topics of a general nature. Here's how it describes itself:

> *PAIS* aims to identify the public affairs information likely to be most useful and interesting to legislators, administrators, the business and financial community, policy researchers and students. The *PAIS* indexes list publications on all subjects that bear on contemporary public issues and the making and evaluation of public policy. . . . This includes the policy-oriented literature of the academic social sciences—economics, political science, public administration, international law and relations, sociology and demography; professional publications in the fields such as business, finance, law, education, and social work; and reports and commentary on public affairs from the serious general press.

As you can see, *PAIS* could be a very important index for topics the general public might be familiar with or wish to know more about. Further, it indexes many more sources than *Readers' Guide* (1,400 versus about 200 for *Readers' Guide*).

Suppose you wondered what was written about mental health. You would want to go through each annual edition of *PAIS*, searching through the appropriate topics. Here's an entry you would find on "Community Mental Health Services" in the 1985 issue:

COMMUNITY MENTAL HEALTH SERVICES

Aldrich, C. Knight. Deinstitutionalization. *Univ Va News Letter* 62:1-5 S '85
   Background and experience in Virginia and nationally of changing the locus of care for the mentally ill and retarded from state-run institutions to the community.

Brown, Phil, ed. Mental health care and social policy. '85 ix+416p bibls tables charts (LC 84-23796) (ISBN 0-7100-9899-5) $42; (ISBN 0-7102-0472-8) pa $19.95
   —*Routledge*
   Reprinted from various sources published between 1971 and 1982.
   United States.

Emerson, Judy. Serving the mentally ill: the Gordian knot of state human services policy. *Ill Issues 11:21-5 N '85*
  Financial and organizational problems; Illinois.

Mangen, Steen P., ed. Mental health care in the European Community. '85 278p bibl tables index (LC 85-6661) (ISBN 0-7099-1755-4) *£16.95 ($29)—*Croom Helm Ltd*

Pettifor, Jean L. Patient rights, professional ethics, and situational dilemmas in mental health services. *Can's Mental Health 33:20-3 S '85*
  Focuses on voluntary clients in community-based mental health care services; Canada.

Look closely at the entry by Aldrich. There's a brief description of the article's topic. *PAIS* does that for almost all entries. That sort of annotation can be really helpful.

Social Sciences Index

The *Social Sciences Index* is part of a family of indexes published by H. W. Wilson Company. This particular one indexes about 250 periodicals covering the following fields:

anthropology
economics
environmental sciences
geography
law and criminology
planning and public administration
political science
psychology
social aspects of medicine
sociology
related subjects

This is a very helpful index because it covers scholarly and special-interest journals, just the sort you'll probably need for your research paper. It's not annotated like *PAIS*, unfortunately, but it is thorough.

For topics on William Faulkner or chemical engineering, you wouldn't find this index of much help, of course, but for the topic of mental depression, you'd find over *120* entries in the April 1984–March 1985 issue. Here's just a small sample:

Depression and old age identification. S. K. Baum and R. L. Boxley. bibl *J Clin Psychol* 39:584-90 Jl '83
Depression, guilt, and self-management of pleasant and unpleasant events. E. H. Wertheim and J. C. Schwarz. bibl *J Pers Soc Psychol* 45:884-9 O '83
Depression in multiple sclerosis as a function of length and severity of illness, age, remissions, and perceived social support. G. P. McIvor and others. bibl *J Clin Psychol* 40:1028-33 Jl '84

You'll have to go to the articles to find out if they're useful, and your library may not have many of the journals available (check your library's listing of periodicals). Still, this long list could be *very* helpful.

Humanities Index

The *Humanities Index* is similar to the *Social Sciences Index* (they're both part of the H. W. Wilson Company's family of indexes) but, of course, it indexes different fields. These are the fields it covers:

archaeology and classical studies
area studies
folklore
history
language and literature
performing arts
philosophy
religion and theology
related subjects

An entry resembles the one we just showed you for the *Social Sciences Index*.

Applied Science and Technology Index

This is another in the H. W. Wilson family of indexes, also very good and very thorough. It indexes periodicals in these fields:

aeronautics and space science
chemistry
computer technology and applications
construction industry
energy resources and research
engineering
fire and fire prevention
food and food industry
geology
machinery
mathematics
metallurgy
mineralogy
oceanography
petroleum and gas
physics
plastics
textile industry and fabrics
transportation
other industrial and mechanical arts

NEWSPAPER INDEXES

Newspapers can be very valuable sources on almost any subject—but how do you locate articles on subjects you're interested in? After all, most newspapers don't publish indexes.

However, one of the best-known newspapers in the country does: *The New York Times Index*. This index has annual volumes, is very complete, and is annotated (which means there's a short description of the article).

Suppose you're interested in what the newspapers were saying about firearms in 1985. When you go to the January to March quarterly index, you find this entry:

FIREARMS. See also
Abortion, Ja 12
Airlines and Airplanes, Ja 2
Cuba, Mr 28
Drug Traffic, Mr 21
Educ, F 14,25
Grenada, F 8,9,16, Mr 1
Hunting and Trapping
Murders, Mr 28
Police, Mr 30
Robberies, Mr 28
Shootings
Transit Systems, Ja 26,27, F 26,28, Mr 28
US Armament, Ja 20
US Pol, F 16
   Italian 9-millimeter Beretta is chosen to replace Colt .45 as standard pistol for US armed forces; Beretta's US division in Accokeek, Md, is given five-year $50 million contract to produce 315,930 guns (S), Ja 15,I,8:6
   British Army is being re-equipped for first time in 20 years, including new SA rifle, 15 inches shorter than predecessor and able to fire standard NATO lightweight 5.56-mm ammunition at very high velocity with almost no recoil; photo (M), F 4,I,3:1
   John Chin, whose arrest ultimately led to resignation of New York City Schools Chancellor Anthony J Alvarado, is convicted of charge of criminal possession of weapon and reckless endangerment (S), F 15,II,7:1
   Three men linked to investigations of arms and drug smuggling are indicted on charges they conspired to take $5.8 million in cash out of US in jet; they are Gus Maestrales, Francisco Rodrigo Guirola-Beeche and Oscar A Rodriguez-Feo (S), F 16,I,15:3
   New York State Senate approves bill easing way for people who legally carry weapons Upstate or on Long Island to bring pistols into New York City (S), Mr 6,II,4:5
   George Gregory Korkala is sentenced to serve 5 to 15 years in prison for plotting to sell 10,000 submachine guns to detectives posing as Latin American terrorists; his co-conspirator, Frank E Terpil, is still fugitive (S), Mr 7,II,6:6
   New York City police officer Willy Rogers shoots himself in finger while trying to unload gun found on Harlem street (S), Mr 18,II,7:6
   Supreme Court, in 8 to 0 decision, rules that individual cannot be convicted and punished for violating two Federal firearms laws when same weapon is involved; Justice Lewis Powell, who is recuperating from surgery, did not participate; one law makes it crime for person previously convicted of felony to 'receive' firearm and other makes it crime to 'possess' firearm; (Ball vs US) (M), Mr 27,I,23:2
   White supremacist Gary Lee Yarbrough, described as chief lieutenant for violent neo-Nazi group, is sentenced Boise, Idaho, to 25 years in prison on Federal firearms and explosives possession charges; Federal District Judge Harold Ryan also sentences Yarbrough to five years' probation for shooting at three Federal agents; police say one of weapons found in Yarbrough's home was submachine gun believed used to kill Denver radio talk-show host Alan Berg (M), Mr 30,I,7:4

The codes *(S)*, *(M)*, and *(L)* tell whether the article is short, medium, or long. Most colleges and some municipal libraries have *The New York Times* itself on microfilm or microfiche, often going back many years into the past. And *The New York Times* is more than just a good source for events; it also has many fine essays and editorials.

The New York Times also can be a key to other newspapers: Once you find an event in *The New York Times Index* or in the newspaper itself—say, the date the pole vault took place in the 1936 Olympics—you can turn to the same date in another paper and perhaps find a related article.

BIBLIOGRAPHIES

Bibliographies are lists of sources for given topics. We discuss bibliographies later in this chapter (under "Other Sources") because they seldom are limited to articles in periodicals. Most bibliographies, however, include articles in periodicals, often covering quite a range of periodicals. And some list works for such large, general topics that they become difficult to distinguish from indexes. For example, the *MLA International Bibliography,* which we illustrate later, includes material on language and literature (a rather broad topic) from well over 2,000 journals and books with essays each year. The number of periodicals screened for this large bibliography, then, is greater than that covered in any of the general indexes we've just discussed. So when you're looking for articles in periodicals, never rule out the bibliographies.

ABSTRACTS

Remember the annotations—brief descriptions of the contents of articles—that *PAIS* gives? There's a special reference tool that goes a step further and gives an abstract, which is a longer summary, of articles. As with the indexes above, these abstracts are for articles for the most part. Not every discipline has abstracts, unfortunately, but for history you could go to *Historical Abstracts,* or for psychology to *Psychological Abstracts.* Here's a sample entry from *Psychological Abstracts:*

> Among variables investigated with regard to age, sex, and time comparisons were types of drugs used, purpose of ingestions, medical condition on arrival, disposition after emergency care, and history of treatment for emotional problems. Results show a continuing escalation (1,050%) in drug overdose emergencies, over 80% of which were related to intentional self-poisoning. Other findings include (a) higher overdose rate at younger ages and among females; (b) barbiturates, analgesics, and tranquilizers as the most common types of drugs used; (c) recent surge in admissions related to drug use for hedonistic reasons; (d) increasing frequency of multiple drug ingestion and combined ingestion of alcohol and drugs; and (e) fre-

quent history of prior psychiatric treatment for emotional problems.—
Journal abstract.

This summary could help you decide whether to look for the article itself; as a general rule, you wouldn't use an abstract as a source for your paper. If your library doesn't have the journal, the abstract can help you decide whether to ask your librarian to order a copy from another library.

BIBLIOGRAPHY CARDS FOR PERIODICALS

When you're making working bibliography cards for books, you list only the key information from the card in the card catalog. However, you might as well list all the information you can find for periodicals while you're still at the index—in other words, before you've actually seen the periodical or found out if it's even in the library. The reason is simple: You'll need most of the bibliographic information to find the periodical, anyway. Here's what a working bibliography card would look like for the sample entry we discussed in the *Readers' Guide:*

```
                                              BE

    Bennett, F. C.
    "APS Fuel-Cycle Study Finds
     Nuclear Technology Sound"
    Physics Today
    30: 77-9 (July 1977)
```

Usually the volume number is sufficient for finding the source in the library, but having the date on the working bibliography card can be important. Sometimes sources on shelves or in the microfilm/microfiche section of the library are identified more easily by the date than by the volume number. In addition, later when you write the Works Cited entries for your final paper, you may need the volume number, the issue number, and the date or only the date, depending on the type of periodical you're documenting.

The information you have on the working bibliography card may not be enough for the parenthetical references and Works Cited pages of your final paper. Therefore, when you find an article you think you may use, copy down everything you can find about the volume and issue numbers, date, or whatever the periodical uses to identify itself. If you have recorded a name like the "Bennett, F. C." in our sample, check to see whether the article is signed with only initials or whether it actually has the full name. And notice whether the periodical is paginated continuously throughout a volume or independently issue by issue. For example, if issue 2 of a volume ends with page 643 and issue 3 of the same volume begins with page 644, the publication paginates issues continuously throughout a volume. If the issues each start with page 1, then the issues are paginated independently. The distinction between continuous and independent pagination will not matter as you conduct your research, but it will help you decide which format to use when you write Works Cited entries. You probably will not need all the information you record on the working bibliography card for your parenthetical references and Works Cited section, but this way you will not have to try to find the periodical again when you are trying to finish your paper. (Again, Chapters 9–12 cover the various documentation systems, all of which use some form of the Works Cited entries in Chapter 10.)

OTHER SOURCES

There are some other sources that may be helpful in finding material for your research paper.

BIBLIOGRAPHIES

A bibliography is a list of sources for a topic, sometimes sources *by someone* (such as the novels and short stories *by* William Faulkner) and sometimes the sources *about someone or something* (such as critical articles and books *about* William Faulkner). Indexes contain many "bibliographies"; the sample you saw in *Readers' Guide* on "mental depression" is a small bibliography on that subject, as are the collections of entries under every other subject heading in the indexes. The very reason you use indexes is for the bibliographies they contain. But there are other sources of bibliographies. For example, an index may do more than serve as a bibliography; it also may cite one.

Some bibliographies appear yearly and are very similar to general indexes. If you're looking for material on a topic in language and literature, turn to the *MLA International Bibliography* ("MLA" means "Modern Language Association"). Each year *MLA* covers well over 2,000 journals and books with essays. It organizes articles in these sources into such major categories as French literature, American literature, linguistics, and so forth, and breaks these into smaller and smaller categories until it reaches topics like "Afro-American" American literature or major authors' names like "Faulkner." You can look at the 1984 *MLA* and find just about everything published about language and literature during that year. The 1984 *MLA* has entries for things published in 1984, and so on. Here's a small part of the 1984 *MLA* entry on Raymond Chandler:

CHANDLER, RAYMOND (1888–1959)

Fiction

[9236] Babener, Liahna K. "Raymond Chandler's City of Lies." 109–131 in Fine, David, ed. *Los Angeles in Fiction: A Collection of Original Essays.* Albuquerque: U of New Mexico P; 1984. 262 pp. [†Treatment of Los Angeles as metaphor for deception.]

Novel

[9237] Arden, Leon. "A Knock at the Backdoor of Art: The Entrance of Raymond Chandler." 73–96 in Benstock, Bernard, ed. *Art in Crime Writing: Essays on Detective Fiction.* New York: St. Martin's; 1983. xi, 218 pp. [Detective novel. Includes biographical information.]

[9238] Demouzon, Alain. "Sur un air de paradoxe: A propos du polar noir, de Phil Marlowe et Ray Chandler." *Europe.* 1984 Aug.–Sept.; 664–665: 30–38. [†Detective novel. Treatment of Marlowe, Philip (character).]

[9239] Tani, Stefano. "Philip Marlowe e il sistema degli oggetti." *Ponte.* 1984 Nov.–Dec.; 40(6): 86–110. [†Treatment of objects; relationship to setting; characterization.]

Also, each volume of *MLA* includes *other* bibliographies published in language and literature.

Sometimes bibliographies are published as individual books. Look under the appropriate subject in the card catalog. If there's an entire book that's a bibliography on your subject, a card for it will have "BIBLIOGRAPHY" in the subject heading. Sometimes, too, a book on your subject will have a bibliography at the end. Again, the card catalog will give you a tip:

DS 596.5 .R6
Roff, William R.
    The origins of Malay nationalism, by William R. Roff. New Haven, Yale University Press, 1967.

    xx, 297 p. Illus., facsims., ports. 24 cm. (Yale Southeast Asia studies, 2)

→   Bibliography: p. 260–284.

    1. Nationalism—Malay Peninsula. 2. Elite (Social sciences) 3. Malay Peninsula—Hist. I. Title (Series)
    DS596.5.R6   320.1'58'095951   67–13447
    Library of Congress   [5]

This book has a 25-page bibliography on Malay nationalism.

Many journals also contain bibliographies. A journal covers a specific field anyway, and it may publish a bibliography regularly, such as every quarter or every year.

You may wonder if there is an index to help you find not just articles and books but entire bibliographies. The *Bibliographic Index* serves that purpose. It searches books and about 2,400 periodicals for the bibliographies they contain. A bibliography is listed if it has at least 50 sources. Here's a sample entry:

FAULKNER, William, 1897-1962
by
Meriwether, J. B. Books of William Faulkner; a
guide for students and scholars. Miss Q 30:417-28
Summ '77
about
Kawin, Bruce F. Faulkner and film. Ungar '77 p183-4
by and about
Bungert, Hans. William Faulkner und die humoris-
tische Tradition des amerikanischen Südens.
(Jahrbuch für Amerikastudien. Beihefte, no32)
Winter '71 p227-32

The first entry is a twelve-page list of books by Faulkner—not very helpful if you're interested in Faulkner criticism but perhaps useful if you need a list of Faulkner's works. The second entry is a two-page list of sources about Faulkner and film—again perhaps not much help unless you're working on Faulkner's relation to the film industry. You may not even be able to read the last entry.

For many topics on Faulkner this particular volume of *Bibliographic Index* may not be much help. But it's easy to check, and it potentially offers a valuable list of reference tools for you. It probably should be one of the first places you go after the card catalog.

BIOGRAPHICAL COLLECTIONS

Some of the best sources for the facts of people's lives are collections of biographies. *Current Biography,* for example, has lengthy and very readable essays on living personalities. Consult the index that appears with it every few years to find which yearbook covers the person you are interested in.

Two other good sources, but for deceased persons, are the *Dictionary of American Biography* and the *Dictionary of National Biography* (for the British).

If you're interested in quick facts on living people—such as business people, political leaders, authors—consult *Who's Who* for the British, *Who's Who in America,* or any of the other versions, such as *Who's Who in American Politics, Who's Who in Art, Who's Who and Where in Women's Studies,* and others.

DISSERTATION ABSTRACTS INTERNATIONAL

Like the reference tools we mentioned above that list abstracts, *Dissertation Abstracts International,* often shown as *DAI* in indexes, also contains abstracts. Here, however, the abstracts are summaries of dissertations that graduate students have written. These dissertations almost certainly will not be available in your library, but *DAI* tells how to order printed or microform copies if you have the time.

ENCYCLOPEDIAS

Encyclopedias are excellent for preliminary reading—when you're trying to decide on a topic or beginning to narrow it to something workable. But after that stage, you're almost always better off going to other sources. An exception is the *Encyclopaedia Britannica,* which is known for the quality, depth, and timeliness of its articles. But if you're looking just for general information, any of the popular ones will do.

YOUR REFERENCE LIBRARIAN

One of the best sources available is your reference librarian. You should plan on talking with the reference librarian sometime while you're compiling your bibliography. The librarian can direct you to the specialized index for your topic if there is one. Even if you think you've found just the index you need, you might want to check with the librarian to be sure.

LIST OF SOURCES BY ACADEMIC DISCIPLINE

The appendix at the end of this book lists a number of reference tools under particular academic disciplines. The listings by no means are complete; they're intended only to help you find places to start your research, and they're annotated with comments about their usefulness. The academic fields included are as follows:

aeronautics
agriculture
anthropology
art
astronomy
biology
business
chemistry
computer science
criminology

economics
education
energy studies
engineering
civil engineering
electrical engineering
nuclear engineering
English
environmental studies
film
geography
geology
history
American history
home economics
mathematics
music
nursing
philosophy
physics
political science
psychology
religion
general science
social science
sociology
and theater

COMPUTERS AND THE LIBRARY

So far, we've covered many traditional sources of information in the library: books, journals, indexes, bibliographies, and so forth. All of those existed before the "computer revolution." Has the computer revolution brought about any changes?

Yes—big changes. Computers now affect almost every phase of the library:

- You might use a computerized library card to get into the library, to gain access to photocopying machines, and to check out library material at the circulation desk.
- Instead of moving from shelf to shelf at the card catalog, you might be able to stand at a computer terminal and search the entire library collection by author, title, or subject—and even get a "hard copy" of the results.
- Instead of searching through traditional books for information, you can now get quick access on computer terminals to encyclo-

pedias, dictionaries, and thesauruses. In fact, all of these are easily available on personal computers.

- And instead of compiling a bibliography in the way we've discussed in this chapter, you can have the computer do the work for you.

Obviously, this last point needs elaboration.

You *can* get a computer to search for books and articles that might help with your research project. Many of the indexes, bibliographies, and other reference sources we have mentioned in this chapter (and hundreds we have not mentioned) are on computers. Probably your library can search the right sources and produce a computer listing of books and articles for you—a ready-made working bibliography.

Before you decide the traditional system for compiling a working bibliography is outdated, however, consider some of the advantages and disadvantages of computer searches.

Advantages? A computer search, especially for large projects, can be far faster than the traditional system of going to printed sources and looking through each one carefully. Also, the data bases that computers search may well be more up-to-date than the printed sources—updating a computerized data base requires only a few strokes on a keyboard, doing away with the printing, mailing, sorting, shelving, and so forth, that a printed source requires. Finally, there are some data bases that are available only on computers.

Disadvantages? Computer searches cost money—even if the computer doesn't find anything for you. They also often take several days to get the results, unless you pay extra money to get a printout immediately, which may not always be possible. Third, you are much less self-sufficient with a computer search since you almost certainly have to have an expert reference librarian do the actual searching for you. And finally, since computers are not only very smart but also very dumb, you have to be extremely careful what words you have the computer search for.

What do these advantages and disadvantages translate to in practical terms? Normally, you won't want to bother with a computer search for routine papers; the trouble will probably not be worth the effort. But for large projects—or important projects when you want to find everything possible—then a computer search is the answer.

In fact, you might want to try a computer search for a small project just to see how one works and what it can produce for you. Your library probably has a handout that tells you just what the procedures are.

COMPILING YOUR BIBLIOGRAPHY: A REVIEW

We've covered a lot of material in this chapter. Let's review the process for compiling a bibliography.

First, look in the card catalog for subject cards on your topic. For each source that looks promising, write the call number, author, and title on a 3 × 5 index card. Stay alert for other subject headings and for bibliographies listed in the card catalog. You might also try the *Essay and General Literature Index* for essays within books and the *Bibliographic Index* for possible subject bibliographies in books or periodicals.

When you have enough sources (just one or two if you still need to do some preliminary reading), go to the shelves and start reviewing the books to see if they are helpful. If so, complete your bibliography cards. Watch for footnotes or lists of references that can lead you to subject bibliographies, to periodical articles, or to other books.

When you've been through the books and anything you may have found in *Bibliographic Index,* look for periodical articles. Start with the most specific index you can. For literature, you probably will want to start with *MLA.* For a popular topic, try *PAIS.* For a fairly general or somewhat popular topic, try the *Social Sciences Index,* the *Humanities Index,* or the *Applied Science and Technology Index.* At some point, check with your reference librarian to be sure you're consulting the right indexes.

When an index lists an article that looks helpful, fill out a 3 × 5 card with the complete bibliographic information. Be sure to use the complete title for the periodical rather than an abbreviation. Consult the list of periodicals for your library to see whether the ones you want are available; then find the issues you need. When you read a periodical that looks useful, complete the bibliography card (adding whatever you need to identify the source fully).

If you're working on a topic of general interest or one based on an event that took place within the last century or so, you probably should consult *The New York Times. The New York Times Index* will lead you to the material you are after.

While you're in the research process, you'll want to keep your bibliography cards in several stacks so you can tell what you've already taken notes from, what you still need to locate, and so forth.

As you consult these sources, you will begin to take notes. We have a recommended procedure for that process, too, as you will see in the next chapter.

EXERCISES

A. Does your library use the Dewey Decimal System, the Library of Congress System, or both?

B. Use the following card to answer questions 1–4:

```
BX        Regan, Joseph W
1656            The Philippines: Christian bulwark in Asia.
.R4         Maryknoll,  N.Y.,  Maryknoll  Publications
            [1957]

            41 p. 25 cm. (World horizon reports. Report no. 21)

            Includes bibliography.




            1. Catholic Church in the Philippine Islands. 2. Phil-
        ippine Islands—Church history. I. Title.
        BX1656.R4        [266.2] 279.14        58-1393

        Library of Congress        [2]
```

1. Is this an author, title, or subject card?

2. Who published the book?

3. Under what subjects could you expect to find this book listed in the card catalog?

4. What item on this card is especially important to someone compiling a bibliography?

C. Which of the following are in your library?

1. *Readers' Guide to Periodical Literature*

2. *Essay and General Literature Index*

3. *PAIS Bulletin*

4. *Social Sciences Index*

5. *Humanities Index*

6. *Applied Science and Technology Index*

7. *Psychological Abstracts*

8. *New York Times Index*

9. *The New York Times* on microfilm or microfiche

10. *MLA International Bibliography*

11. *Bibliographic Index*

12. *Current Biography*

13. *Who's Who in America*

14. *Dissertation Abstracts International*

15. *Encyclopaedia Britannica*

D. Use the key in the front of *MLA* to translate the following entry listed under Faulkner in the 1977 volume:

   8965. McCarron, William E. "Shakespeare, Faulkner and Ned William McCaslin." *NConL* 7. v:8–9.

E. In July 1974, a periodical carried an article on the views of R. Heinlein, a science fiction author. Using *Readers' Guide* and the periodical it refers to, answer the following:

1. What periodical carried the article?

2. What college did Heinlein attend and how do you know?

F. In the 1978 *New York Times Index,* at the very end of the section on "Atomic Energy and Weapons—United States—Nuclear Wastes," is a reference to articles on "Subsurface Blasts." Prepare a bibliography card for the article that has comments by David Jackson.

G. Find the front page for October 20, 1977, of *The New York Times.* Using the article at the bottom of the page, tell how much noisier the Concorde is than the noisiest subsonic jets.

H. Assume that while preparing a paper on public health nursing you come across a book called *Hazards of Public Health Nursing in Maine* by Cynthia A. Larsen, R.N. The call number is RM/9791/.A22/B47. The book, published by Stephen David Press in Chicago, has a 1984 copyright, and the third printing was in 1986. Prepare a full working bibliography card, including the code and a remark that the book has many good examples.

4 Evaluating Your Sources and Taking Notes

Once you've made a list of the books and articles you would like to find, and once you've actually found some of them, your next two steps are these: to evaluate those sources to see if they might be useful, and, if they are useful, to take notes on them. This chapter will help you with those two steps.

First, though, let's distinguish two types of research material: *primary sources* and *secondary sources.* Understanding these terms can help you evaluate your sources and know how they can be useful to you.

PRIMARY AND SECONDARY SOURCES

Some sources are more valuable than others. Experienced researchers, for example, often like to use *primary sources* whenever possible.

A **primary source** is the original source of basic facts on your subject. If you're writing about the first people to climb the Matterhorn in 1865, a newspaper interview of one of the climbers would be a primary source.

A **secondary source,** as implied, is secondhand, one or more steps removed from the primary source. It uses primary sources (or even other secondary sources) as its basis. So a newspaper article about the climb—by someone who didn't make the climb personally—would be a secondary source.

Here are some other examples:

Table 1.   Primary and Secondary Sources

Primary Sources	Secondary Sources
novel, poem, or story	critical articles explaining them
Napoleon's diary	biography of Napoleon
transcript of a trial	article in *Newsweek* about that trial

The distinction is not always simple, though. An 1867 newspaper article about the 1865 Matterhorn accident would have been considered a secondary source at the time it was published. Now, though, we might call it a primary source because it was written at a time much closer to the accident and might capture the views of people then.

The importance, therefore, is not in neatly classifying sources as primary or secondary but in recognizing that there are two kinds of material available to you. Here are some of the advantages and disadvantages of each.

Since a primary source gives you the basic material on a topic, you're less likely to be affected by the biases of others who have filtered the material before presenting it. If, for instance, you're working with the transcript of a trial (a primary source), *you* can decide whether the prosecutor's case is sound by tracing the arguments yourself. But if you're reading about the trial in a secondary source—such as a popular or technical article—that source may slant your thinking by pointing out the "brilliance" of the prosecutor's case. Worse, the secondary source may exercise selectivity and point out only the parts of the trial that favor the prosecutor. Without a primary source, you would have no way of knowing what you were missing. So one *advantage* of primary sources is that you get the "unfiltered truth." A *disadvantage* of primary sources is the same thing: You get the "unfiltered truth" and have to do all the spadework—the selecting, the filtering, the evaluating, the analyzing—yourself.

Our recommendation? Try to find as many primary sources as you can. If writing about a topic that has some experts near you, try arranging an interview, thus creating your own primary source. Such an interview could well be the highlight of both your research and your research paper.

But look for secondary sources, too. Each type of source—primary and secondary—has its own strengths and weaknesses. And each type can help you evaluate the other type. Details from primary sources can help you determine the value of secondary sources; the secondary sources, on the other hand, can help you understand the primary sources by telling you what to look for.

EVALUATING YOUR SOURCES

Just how good is that book or article or other source that you've found? Can you really use it for your research project?

First, you need to decide if your potential source is *relevant*—if it really has something significant to do with your topic. Then you have to decide if the source is *reliable*—can you trust what it says?

RELEVANT MATERIAL

Sometimes, since titles can be ambiguous or vague, you can't be sure that the sources listed in the card catalog, indexes, and bibliographies are really about your topic. You will, therefore, need to be something of a detective. For example, suppose you have decided to look into the safety methods (the use of ropes and other equipment) of the early mountaineers to see whether their safety methods were really safe or just another unintended hazard.

In the card catalog you find a listing for *Hours of Exercise in the Alps* by John Tyndall. The catalog card is evidence that the book possibly is related somehow to your topic, but is the work a nineteenth-century physical-fitness treatise or is it a book about mountain climbing?

When you actually have the book in your hands, you confirm that it does deal with the general topic of mountain climbing, but how can you find out if it has specific information on your topic: the supposed safety practices of early mountaineers?

First, of course, check the table of contents. Maybe there will be a chapter on "Climbing Techniques" or something similar. If there is not (and there is no such chapter in this case), next check the introductory material: The preface, author's introduction, or foreword may tell you the range of material covered in the book and the author's intent.

In the preface to this book, *Hours of Exercise in the Alps*, you find out that the author did *not* intend to cover safety techniques:

> I refrain from giving advice, further than to say that the perils of wandering in the High Alps are terribly real, and are only to be met by knowledge, caution, skill, and strength. "For rashness, ignorance, or carelessness the mountains leave no margin; and to rashness, ignorance, or carelessness three-fourths of the catastrophes which shock us are to be traced." Those who wish to know something of the precautions to be taken upon the peaks and glaciers cannot do better than consult the excellent little volume lately published by Leslie Stephen, where, under the head "Dangers of Mountaineering," this question is discussed.[1]

---

[1] John Tyndall, *Hours of Exercise in the Alps* (New York, 1896) vi–vii.

You decide to make a partial bibliography card on Leslie Stephen's book and hope it's available, but don't give up on *Hours of Exercise* yet. Check the index under such possible headings as "ropes," "ice axes," "accidents," and so on, to see what you can find.

Again, there doesn't appear to be much, but you do discover this interesting passage:

> Why, then, it may be asked, employ the rope? The rope, I reply, notwithstanding all its possible drawbacks under such circumstances [one fall could carry all others on the rope to their deaths], is the safeguard of the climber. Not to speak of the moral [psychological] effect of its presence, an amount of help upon a dangerous slope that might be measured by the gravity of a few pounds is often of incalculable importance; and thus, though the rope may be not only useless but disastrous if the footing be clearly lost, and the glissade [slide] fairly begun, it lessens immensely the chance of this occurrence.[2]

This is not the sort of detailed discussion you had hoped for, but Tyndall's paragraph is actually an important aside that shows the philosophy early mountaineers had toward rope use.

In fact, this aside shows something *very* important to you: The supposed safety equipment of early mountaineers could lead, as Tyndall says, to *disaster*. So Tyndall's aside helps answer the question you started your research with: Were the safety methods of the early mountaineers really safe or just another unintended hazard? Perhaps they were another unintended hazard. The extra effort on Tyndall's book was worthwhile.

RELIABLE MATERIAL

Once you find a relevant source, you have to ask yourself, "Can I trust this author?" Just because something is printed does not make it so. If an author says something that doesn't seem convincing to you, trust your intuition and investigate further.

How do you know when to be suspicious? You should always be a little suspicious, but be especially so if the tone of the book—the personality the author projects—raises questions. For example, consider these two forewords to books on the Alamo. Which book would you trust more?

The first foreword is from *A Time to Stand:*

> These men were all kinds.
> They were farmers, clerks, doctors, lawyers. There was a blacksmith . . . a hatter . . . a house painter . . . a jockey . . . a shoemaker . . . a Baptist preacher. Very few were the frontier type, although one was indeed the greatest bear hunter in all the West. . . .

[2] Tyndall 289–90.

As a group, they had little in common—yet everything. For they were all Americans, sharing together a fierce love of liberty and a deep belief that the time had come to take their stand to keep it.[3]

And now consider this foreword from *The Alamo:*

Barring versions which may exist in manuscript, this is the first chronicle of the Alamo which seeks to present the story of that historic structure in full. Finding and assembling the necessary parts has been a fascinating but, at the same time, complicated business. Before they could be recognized with sureness, many of the scattered pieces were walked past time and again. Dozens upon dozens of those available were suspect upon discovery because mutually contradictory. The spurious could only be discarded with confidence after months of reviewing and collating.[4]

Does the author of the first foreword seem so dedicated to the noble motives of the Texans (and the glory they deserve) that you find yourself just a bit mistrustful?

In the second foreword, the author seems more proud of the accuracy of his book than of any motives of the Texans. That doesn't mean that his book is reliable, or even necessarily more reliable than the first, but we're more comfortable at this point that we can trust what the second author says in the main text of his book. Of course, we'll continually evaluate its reliability as we're going through it.

TAKING NOTES: TWO WAYS

After you find and evaluate a source, your next step is to keep track of what you have found. With only a short paper to write, especially one that involves almost no research, your solution is easy: You simply remember. But with larger papers and those involving any amount of research, your confidence in your memory may exceed your memory's ability to perform. Therefore, most researchers have developed some systematic way to keep track of the research information they have found. (And, if those researchers are like us, they developed their system after learning the hard way that human memory is all too limited.)

The most commonly taught system for keeping track of research information involves taking notes on note cards. Now some people think of taking notes on note cards as the worst sort of work—suitable for drones, perhaps, but certainly not suitable for human beings with places to go, people to see, and things to do. Others, however, find taking notes

---

[3] Walter Lord, *A Time to Stand* (New York: Harper, 1961) 11. Ellipses are in the original except the one following the word "West."

[4] John Myers Myers, *The Alamo* (New York: Dutton, 1948) 11.

an easier activity, a productive and rewarding way of organizing themselves and of reaching a goal.

We know these different views of note-taking exist because we, ourselves, exemplify them. One of us prefers the standard system using note cards; one prefers a simpler system relying more heavily on a sack of dimes and a copying machine. So we'll explain both systems, and you can choose the one that better fits your personality type. Both systems can work well and have worked well for each of us in the past on book-length research projects.

We'll call the first system "the traditional system" and the second one "the copying machine system"—since it involves putting money in a copying machine.

THE TRADITIONAL SYSTEM

The traditional system of taking notes, devised before the invention of the ubiquitous copying machine, still has many adherents. Essentially, it goes like this:

Let's say that you're in the library and have found a good book on your topic, mountain climbing. After evaluating the source, you decide it's worthwhile (that is, it is both relevant and reliable—as far as you can tell), so your next step is the actual taking of the notes.

We suggest you take your notes on either 4 × 6 or 5 × 8 index cards because they are easy to handle and easy to rearrange. Later, when you're ready to write your paper, you may want to match your research information to your outline. If the information is on note cards, you can arrange the cards so that all the cards for each topic or subtopic are together, even though you may have found the information at different times and from different sources.

The example on the facing page shows you what a note card looks like:

The *subject of card* helps you keep your cards organized while you're conducting your research and may help you later when you're arranging your cards by topics and subtopics for your outline.

The *code* is a handy way to refer to your *bibliography* card—the card we discussed in the last chapter that you made while going through indexes, bibliographies, card catalog, and so on, looking for possible sources. "Wh 2" means this is the second note card you've made on the book by Edward Whymper. You have the bibliographic information (title, publisher, date, and so on) on the bibliography card, so you don't have to write the information again here.

The *page numbers* add information on the note card that you didn't have on the bibliography card—exactly where in the source you got your information.

The identifying information on the card is important but so is the content of the card. You will need to keep track of whether the infor-

subject of card   code

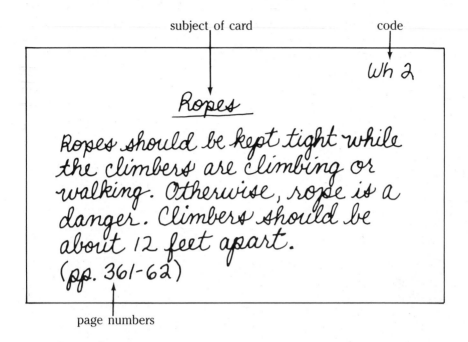

Wh 2

Ropes

Ropes should be kept tight while the climbers are climbing or walking. Otherwise, rope is a danger. Climbers should be about 12 feet apart. (pp. 361-62)

page numbers

mation is a quotation, a paraphrase, a summary, or a mixed quotation and paraphrase/summary.

First, let's define those terms:

- *Quotation:* A quotation is the *exact* words of a source. You put quotation marks around quotations.

- *Paraphrase:* A paraphrase is a restatement, in your own words, of the words in a source. Usually, a paraphrase follows the original organization sentence by sentence. Most times, paraphrases are fairly short.

- *Summary:* A summary is something like a paraphrase: it restates the original in your own words. But a summary also condenses (summarizes), so it's shorter—sometimes considerably shorter—than the original. Another term for "summary" is "précis."

- *Mixed quotation and paraphrase/summary:* This is, as it says, a mixture of the words from the source and your own words. Sometimes you want to summarize or paraphrase a passage but some of the author's words are so good you want to quote them. So you do both: paraphrase (or summarize) and quote. (And you put quotation marks around any quoted material.)

In Chapter 6, we'll tell you how to indicate clearly to your reader when you're quoting or paraphrasing or summarizing in your actual paper. For now, though, let's look at how to keep track of those quotations, paraphrases, and so on, while you're still in the research stage, gathering your material from your sources. For if you're careful at this stage, you can save yourself some time later.

Quotation note card

A quotation note card contains *the exact words, including punctuation, from your source.* You'll be glad to know, as you're writing your paper later, just which note cards contain quotations so that you can give proper credit to the author for those exact words.

While you're still finding sources and gathering research information, you probably don't want to take the time to copy, word for word, the exact words of a long quotation. A copy made on a copying machine with an accompanying note card as a reference might be the answer. A short quotation, on the other hand, won't take long to write down. Having the material on a card to match to your outline could be useful later to remind you not just of the idea of the passage but also of its especially effective wording.

Here's an example of a short passage that would probably be worth copying down by hand. At the end of his account of climbing the Matterhorn, Edward Whymper has a beautifully worded conclusion that you think you might want to quote—at least in part—in your paper. (Whymper was in the first group to climb the Matterhorn, but four of his companions were killed on the descent.) Even though you plan to have the source available, a card with the wording of this particular passage will help you remember to consider quoting it later:

quotation marks

Matterhorn accident   Wh 6

"Others may tread its summit-snows, but none will ever know the feelings of those who first gazed upon its marvelous panorama; and none, I trust, will ever be compelled to tell of joy turned into grief, and of laughter into mourning. It proved to be a stubborn foe; it resisted long   (over) *and gave many a hard blow; it was defeated at last with an ease that none could have anticipated, but, like a relentless enemy -- conquered but not crushed -- it took terrible vengeance."*

(p. 393)

Notice that you use quotation marks to show you've recorded the exact words from your source.

Paraphrase note card

A paraphrase, you'll remember, simply restates a quotation in your own words. Generally, a paraphrase tends to follow the sentence-by-sentence organization of the original and is about the same length.

You should probably use paraphrase note cards sparingly. If you're going to take notes that follow the original as closely as a paraphrase does, why not quote, instead? Then you'll have the exact words in case you decide to quote all or part of the passage in your paper.

Sometimes, though, the original is either highly complex or poorly worded, so a paraphrase can help simplify or "interpret." That's the best time to paraphrase—when you don't need the exact words of the original and want to simplify the wording.

For example, here's a confusing sentence from Tyndall's *Hours of Exercise* (he's talking about the advantage of using a rope while mountain climbing):

> Not to speak of the moral effect of its presence, an amount of help upon a dangerous slope that might be measured by the gravity of a few pounds is often of incalculable importance.

Now, suppose we consider the point of this sentence important enough to keep, but we want to rewrite to simplify the language. The example on the following page shows you what a paraphrase note card might look like:

Notice that you don't, of course, use quotation marks for a paraphrase since you haven't used the *exact* words from your source. Chapter 6 will show you how to give proper credit to the authors you paraphrase.

The difference between a paraphrase note card and a quotation note card is this: The quotation note card, because it contains the exact words from a source, has quotation marks in it.

One caution: When you paraphrase, you must be careful not to mix some exact words from the original—*quoted words*—with your words on a paraphrase note card. If you do need to have some of the words from the original and some of your own words, then you should use a mixed quotation and paraphrase/summary note card. We'll cover that after we discuss the summary note card.

The summary note card

A summary note card looks exactly like a paraphrase note card. In fact, there will be no difference whatsoever in the way you will treat summaries and paraphrases when you actually write your paper. The distinction is useful only as two different ways to think of the notes you're taking: Summaries and paraphrases both change the original to your own wording, but the summary condenses whereas the paraphrase does not.

Let's look at an example of a summary note card. Remember the excerpt earlier in this chapter from *Hours of Exercise* about the use of mountaineering ropes? The wording wasn't particularly effective; it was both verbose and confusing. So you would probably want to use a summary note card, like this:

> *In the 1800's, the climbers thought the ropes would help prevent falls by steadying mountain climbers who had lost their balance. However, the rope could be fatal to all tied to it if a climber actually fell.*
>
> *(pp. 289-90)*
>
> Ty 3

Even if you kept the source at hand or reproduced the page, this summary note card, which condenses the ninety-two words of the original to thirty-five words, would provide a quick reminder of the essence of the material and would tell you where to find the original if you need it later.

Mixed quotation and paraphrase or summary note card

You need to be very careful when you are paraphrasing or summarizing that you don't accidentally quote key words of phrases without using quotation marks. As we explain in Chapter 6, presenting the exact words of an author—even as little as a key word or phrase—without giving credit is plagiarism. Whether it is intentional or unintentional, plagiarism must be avoided.

So how do you give the proper credit? Let's look at the example on the following page. Here is an original passage—the same one we already paraphrased—and then a mixed paraphrase and quotation note card taken from it. Notice that we've put the key words in quotation marks.

Summary of the traditional system (making note cards)

For the traditional system of keeping track of your sources, find a source and then take notes about it on note cards. Making these cards has several important benefits:

- You have had to actively engage your mind with the material by taking the notes, so it becomes something you understand better

Ty 3

Even if one sets aside its psychological effect, a rope can be of "incalculable importance" when a slight steadying pressure is necessary.

(p. 289)

than if you had only glanced through it—or even read it carefully.
- You have organized your process so you can easily tell what you have found and what you have not found.
- You can rearrange the cards later to match your outline.
- You can even tape the notes onto the actual draft of your paper, thus saving writing or typing time.

Those are substantial benefits, but they come at the cost of being painstaking while you are reviewing the material. For some people, the benefits outweigh the pain. For others, however, the pain outweighs the benefits. The next section is for the second group of people.

THE COPYING MACHINE SYSTEM

Suppose you are reading an interesting article that looks useful for your paper. Should you stop and take notes, thus interrupting your train of thought? If you do stop, and particularly if you stop frequently, you may have trouble staying with the main ideas of the article and get lost from the constant stops and starts. If you don't stop to take notes, however, you may permanently forget that small but significant point you just read.

If the last paragraph seems to describe you, you might consider this method: When you find an article that looks worthwhile, make a copy of it. Then, as you read it, use a *highlighting* pen to mark anything you want to be able to refer to later. Be sure when you copy the article that you have complete bibliographic information (just write it on the front page of the copy you make). For a book, simply copy the pages you find useful and then highlight the parts you wish to remember. Please do not ever highlight the library copy (a practice which would be rude and probably is illegal, or should be).

Can you keep track of your sources as well this way as with note cards? No. But you *can* keep track well enough if you keep all the highlighted material together. You won't be able to shuffle it as you would note cards, but, then again, you didn't have to distract yourself and spend extra time taking notes at the beginning of the process.

Both the traditional system and the copying machine system can work. The "system" that doesn't work is no system at all: some random reading combined with misplaced confidence in human memory.

EVOLVING A WORKING OUTLINE

We talk more about outlining in the next chapter, which covers the writing process, but we also need to talk briefly about outlines here. Should you make an outline for your research paper? And if so, when?

Unless you decide to write a very creative research paper—and such papers can be enjoyable to read, enjoyable to write, and valuable all the way around—you will almost certainly want to develop some sort of an outline.

You don't need anything formal. For papers in the past, you may have scribbled a few notes to yourself before you started writing. *But, for a research paper, a more substantial outline can save you a terrific amount of time and energy.*

Start by writing a tentative outline as soon as you can, perhaps even before you get beyond the preliminary research stage we talked about in Chapter 2. That way, you will have some direction for your research: an idea of what will be relevant for you and what will not be.

The following could be a tentative outline at a very early stage of the research process:

WORKING THESIS: The "safety precautions" of early mountain climbers were actually more dangerous than safe.

ONE POSSIBLE TOPIC: The climbing *equipment* was dangerous.

ANOTHER POSSIBLE TOPIC: The climbing *techniques* were dangerous.

See how this can help you focus your research?

Now here's the real key: Keep a copy of your working outline with you, and whenever you read something that could fit, actually jot it down on the outline. After just a little research, your working outline might look like this:

> WORKING THESIS: The "safety precautions" of early mountain climbers were actually more dangerous than safe.
>> ONE POSSIBLE TOPIC: The climbing *equipment* was dangerous.
>> (see Tyndall, p. 289—talks about ropes)
>> (see Whymper, p. 43)
>> (consider Carpenter—pitons were badly made)
>> (I wonder if the boots had good soles?)
>> ANOTHER POSSIBLE TOPIC: The climbing *techniques* were dangerous.
>> (see Stephens—mentioned by Tyndall, vi–vii)
>> (Coyne mentions in *Climbing* Aug 82, p. 56)
>> (did they know how to belay?)

See the advantages? The outline helps you keep track of what you've found and what you need. This system in combination with either the note card system or the copying machine system can be quite powerful.

What if you find something important and interesting that doesn't fit your outline? Remember that you can always change the outline. Perhaps you started your research knowing little about your topic. Certainly you knew *less* or you haven't really done much research. As you do your research, then, and as you find out more about your topic, you need to allow your original outline to change. That is why we called it a *tentative* outline.

So we recommend you stop every now and then as you conduct your research and think through your outline again. And if you need to change it, then do so. Also, you might ask your instructor for comments.

If you use this system of outlining, what will you have when you finish your research? You will have a document you definitely will not want to lose. It will contain the complete flow of your paper along with all of your research information—identified, organized, and listed under each topic. With something like that, you will be ready to write. We cover the fundamentals of writing your paper in the next chapter.

EXERCISES

A. Give an example of a primary source and a secondary source based on it (you do not need specific titles).

Primary source _____

Secondary source _____

B. Here's a passage from *Walden* by Henry David Thoreau. Use it for items 1–3 below.

> No man ever stood the lower in my estimation for having a patch in his clothes; yet I am sure that there is greater anxiety, commonly, to have fashionable, or at least clean and unpatched clothes, than to have a sound conscience. But even if the rent is not mended, perhaps the worst vice betrayed is improvidence. I sometimes try my acquaintances by such tests as this: Who could wear a patch, or two extra seams only, over the knee? Most behave as if they believed that their prospects for life would be ruined if they should do it. It would be easier for them to hobble to town with a broken leg than with a broken pantaloon.

1. Make a quotation note card using the last sentence from the selection above.

2. Now make a mixed paraphrase and quotation card using that same sentence.

3. Make a brief summary card using the entire passage. You don't need to capture every idea—just what you consider important.

C. Here is another passage from *Walden*. Use it to answer items 1 and 2 below.

> But men labor under a mistake. The better part of the man is soon plowed into the soil for compost. By a seeming fate, commonly called necessity, they are employed, as it says in an old book, laying up treasures which moth and rust will corrupt and thieves break through and steal. It is a fool's life, as they will find when they get to the end of it, if not before.

1. Make a quotation note card using the second sentence.

```
┌─────────────────────────────────────────────────────────┐
│                                                           │
│                                                           │
│                                                           │
│                                                           │
│                                                           │
│                                                           │
│                                                           │
│                                                           │
│                                                           │
│                                                           │
│                                                           │
│                                                           │
│                                                           │
└─────────────────────────────────────────────────────────┘
```

2. Make a brief summary card for the entire passage. Again, you do not need to capture every idea—just what you consider important.

```
┌─────────────────────────────────────────────────────────┐
│                                                           │
│                                                           │
│                                                           │
│                                                           │
│                                                           │
│                                                           │
│                                                           │
│                                                           │
│                                                           │
│                                                           │
│                                                           │
│                                                           │
│                                                           │
└─────────────────────────────────────────────────────────┘
```

D. In Exercise C for Chapter 2, you chose a proposed topic for a research paper. Using either that topic or the one you actually are using for your paper, prepare a tentative outline. Follow the format we presented in this chapter.

5

Some Fundamentals of Writing: The Process and the Product

In this chapter we will cover some of the fundamentals of writing that are particularly important for research papers. We'll start by suggesting a writing process that many successful writers—from students to professionals—find effective, even crucial to their success. Then we'll show you what a typical research paper could look like and discuss the various parts of it in more detail.

THE WRITING PROCESS

What do we mean by "the writing process"? It's the process you go through to get words on paper, the way you and other people proceed from an idea to a final product. There's no one right way, no single writing process, but recent research shows that good writing processes often have many similarities.

In the past, writing teachers divided the writing process into three stages: prewriting, writing, and rewriting. Writing teachers today do the same thing, but there are two differences: Today's writing teachers would probably tell you different things to do in each of those stages. And today's writing teachers would caution you that writing does not usually progress linearly—in lock-step order from prewriting, then to writing, and then to rewriting.

Actually, the process is more recursive. Good writers move generally from prewriting to writing to rewriting, but are constantly looping back and forth in the process, doing a little prewriting when in the writing stage, doing some writing when in the rewriting stage, and so forth. In reality, writers rarely move neatly from prewriting to writing to rewriting.

With that caution in mind, then, let's go ahead and consider the writing process as divided into the three stages of *prewriting, writing,* and *rewriting.* Just remember that the writing process is really somewhat recursive.

PREWRITING

Think of prewriting as the stage of *preparing* for that session (or those sessions) when you'll be doing the actual writing of the paper. During prewriting, you want to come up with a topic (which Chapter 2 helped you with), do your research (which Chapters 3 and 4 helped you with), and end up with everything you need either on paper in front of you (for example, on note and bibliography cards) or in your head, or both.

For short, relatively uncomplicated papers, keeping everything in your head is usually no problem. But for many research papers, most of us don't have the photographic memories required to keep *all* research material in our heads. That's why the bibliography card and note-taking processes we discussed in Chapters 3 and 4 are important. So one key to good prewriting for research papers is to be a good ''bookkeeper.''

Another key to good prewriting is to outline your paper, which we discussed in the last chapter. If you can develop a working outline early and constantly jot down key sources in the right places on the outline, you can be miles ahead when you start the writing stage.

We suggest, however, that you ignore advice to stick to your outline no matter what. Think of your outline as a way of tentatively organizing yourself for the writing stage, as a way of collecting all your ideas in a skeletal form, but not as something etched in bronze that will limit the creative thinking you could do in the writing stage. Let's talk about this point more, because it's significant.

Have you ever had ideas that you hadn't thought of during the prewriting stage occur to you while you were actually writing? That happens all the time to experienced writers, who value those ideas and try to construct a writing process that will allow—even encourage—those inspirations to happen.

If you haven't had those inspirations while writing, you've certainly had them while speaking: How often, when you're talking to somebody, do you even know how you'll end the sentence you're speaking? Not often. You have probably found that some really interesting ideas occurred to you *while you were talking.* That's the kind of experience you need to encourage while you're *writing.*

How do you *prevent* that experience from happening? You make the mistake of outlining your paper from beginning to end during the prewriting stage and then doggedly sticking to that outline no matter what when you're writing the paper. That way you put a straitjacket on your mind, not allowing it to wander, to discover new thoughts, new connections that didn't occur during prewriting.

How do you *help* that experience to happen? You do two things: First, you outline your paper as much as you can, finding ways to organize your writing so it will make sense to your reader (and to you). Then, with your outline in hand, you just start writing.

WRITING

This is where the rubber meets the road—where you find out if you really have a paper. We suggest you begin by immersing yourself in your subject by looking carefully at your outline and reviewing your important sources briefly. And then just start writing.

Imagine you're simply talking to your reader (to your instructor, perhaps? or to your class?), telling him or her what you want to say.

If you're writing an informative paper, imagine yourself simply telling your reader (conscious of your need to be organized, of course) what you've learned. That's what we have tried to do in this book.

If you're writing a persuasive paper, imagine yourself gently persuading your reader (again, conscious of your need to be organized) what you believe to be true.

Now we will give you some advice on using the outline during this stage of the writing process. You prepared the outline during the prewriting stage to help you collect and organize your thoughts. We suggest you keep a pretty tight organization at the more general level of your paper: Divide your paper into several parts, and, if possible, stick to them. But once you get within a part of your paper, consult your outline to remind yourself of the points you would like to cover, and then just write. Don't worry too much about being completely organized down to the paragraph level. If you've organized your paper at the more general level, and if you imagine yourself talking on paper to your reader, you do two things:

- You'll stay much more organized than you might think.
- You'll allow those inspirations to happen that we mentioned at the beginning of the paper.

What do you then do with those inspirations when they occur? Obviously you hadn't accounted for them during your prewriting stage, so you may have ruined a perfectly good outline. Our advice is to trust your inspirations. That's why you need to think of your outline as "a suggested organization to start with." And that's why we suggest that you outline—but not too much.

Work with your inspirations rather than denying them, and trust that your best ideas will probably occur with the pen in your hand (or, even better, with your hands on the computer keyboard). When you're actually writing, rather than thinking about writing, your mind is actively, closely engaged with your topic and struggling to capture ideas with those elusive things: words. Many good ideas happen at this time. Inspiration, you see, is not a gift from the gods but, rather, a gift from your own mind.

REWRITING

Too often, students think of rewriting as simply fixing errors: correcting punctuation, spelling words correctly, and catching typos.

Rewriting is all of those things, of course, but experienced writers consider these things, too, during the rewriting stage:

Is my paper interesting throughout?
Are there places where I have not been clear?
Is my organization the best?
Have I used enough details so that my reader can see what I mean?
Are there places where I've been too wordy?
Do my ideas follow logically from one to the next?
Does my layout (the size of paragraphs and the appearance of the page) seem inviting?
Have I chosen my words carefully?

Although rewriting is a time to fix errors, it is also a time to be sure that your paper makes sense—that it works for your reader in all ways.

THE PARTS OF THE PAPER

All research papers do not look alike. We tend to think of them as having an introduction, a body, and a conclusion, but some of the best research writing is much more creative. Let's consider two beginnings that were written by professional writers who were writing books that involved considerable research. You will be able to tell from these beginnings that the structure of the research writing is far from typical.

Here are the very first sentences from John McPhee's best-seller, *Coming into the Country*, a book about contemporary Alaska:

My bandanna is rolled on the diagonal and retains water fairly well. I keep it knotted around my head, and now and again dip it into the river. The water is forty-six degrees.[1]

Notice that McPhee seems to be talking to us (as we recommended in the previous section of this chapter). Notice also that his is not a standard introduction.

[1] (New York: Farrar, 1977) 5.

Here are the first five sentences from Tom Wolfe's *The Electric Kool-Aid Acid Test,* a book about the drug society in California in the 1960s:

> That's good thinking there, Cool Breeze. Cool Breeze is a kid with three or four days' beard sitting next to me on the stamped metal bottom of the open back part of a pickup truck. Bouncing along. Dipping and rising and rolling on these rotten springs like a boat. Out the back of the truck the city of San Francisco is bouncing down the hill, all those endless staggers of bay windows, slums with a view, bouncing and streaming down the hill.[2]

Again, notice that this doesn't seem like a standard introduction and that it seems as if the writer is talking to us.

These two excerpts are from highly successful books by highly successful authors who frequently write books based on extensive research.

Can you write your paper in that style? Well, you should feel free to try. There's nothing that says a research paper has to be dull. In fact, these two writers are obviously trying very hard to be as engaging as possible, and we think they succeed.

On the other hand, there are times when a more straightforward organization is preferable. Most technical and business writing—the kind you're likely to do outside of college—tends to follow the traditional formula of "tell them what you're going to tell them (the introduction), tell them (the main points), then tell them what you told them (the conclusion)." Despite the fact that we've all heard it many times before, it's a good formula and one that need not result in papers that are boring to writers and readers alike.

So although we acknowledge the creative research paper can be an extremely fine one and although we do not want to discourage you from trying that style, we will now show you the type of organization that research papers have traditionally followed.

THE OVERALL ORGANIZATION

On the facing page is a model showing the organization of a standard research paper, one that can successfully communicate in a straightforward way to a reader.

You may have as many main points as you wish, of course. And each main point could be a paragraph, or a page, or ten pages, or a chapter. We're simply showing you a model that can apply regardless of the length.

Within the main point sections, you may wish to have some subsections, depending on the length of your paper. How far you carry this

---

[2] (New York: Bantam, 1968) 1.

```
┌─────────────────────────────────┐
│                                 │
│                                 │
│          INTRODUCTION           │
│                                 │
│                                 │
└─────────────────────────────────┘

┌─────────────────────────────────┐
│                                 │
│                                 │
│        FIRST  MAIN  POINT       │
│                                 │
│                                 │
└─────────────────────────────────┘

┌─────────────────────────────────┐
│                                 │
│                                 │
│       SECOND  MAIN  POINT       │
│                                 │
│                                 │
└─────────────────────────────────┘

┌─────────────────────────────────┐
│                                 │
│        THIRD  MAIN  POINT       │
│             (etc.)              │
│                                 │
└─────────────────────────────────┘

┌─────────────────────────────────┐
│                                 │
│                                 │
│           CONCLUSION            │
│                                 │
│                                 │
└─────────────────────────────────┘
```

organization—down to the paragraph level, for example—is up to you. At some point, you may just wish to write about a section or subsection without worrying about the organization.

Now let's look at the individual parts of this model. (You can find a specific example of each part in Chapter 7, "A Sample Research Paper.")

THE INTRODUCTION

An introduction should serve two functions: gaining the reader's interest and stating the topic of the paper clearly. The excerpts we just quoted by McPhee and Wolfe certainly gain the reader's interest, though McPhee and Wolfe never state, explicitly, their overall purposes. Then again, their purposes are quite different from yours.

A good way to begin a paper is with an intriguing fact you learned in your research: "Did you know that the soldiers who died in the Alamo probably would have been court-martialed for insubordination if they had survived?" Or try to think of something relevant to your paper that will genuinely intrigue the reader.

A good way to state the topic of your paper clearly is to use the thesis sentence you developed as you did your research (Chapter 2 discussed how to develop a good thesis sentence). You may wish to reword it to fit it into the context of your introduction, however.

THE MAIN POINTS

This section is generally self-explanatory, but there are two special considerations.

First, be sure the reader knows unmistakably that you've moved from one main point to the next. For longer papers, you can accomplish this goal easily by using headings. We use them frequently in this book, and we explain them in Chapter 14. You will also wish to state your main point clearly near the beginning of the first paragraph of that section:

> We've looked at some reasons the soldiers might have been guilty of insubordination. Now consider some reasons they might not have been guilty. . . .

Second, be sure to use support for your main point that is detailed enough for your reader to understand what you're saying. One common problem with any college writing is that the support is too general.

Let's consider an example. Suppose you want to show that the Olympics around the turn of the century had controversies that produced international bitterness. During your research, you read that the English officials in the 1908 Olympics were blatantly biased against the Americans. A poor writer, one who wrote mainly in generalities, would probably leave out colorful details and make only a bland point such as this:

> The way the English Officials handled the 1908 marathon was very controversial since they were obviously biased against an American competitor. For example, officials helped the Italian competitor so that the American wouldn't win.

The writer left out all the thrill of the race and the heat of the controversy. A better writer could have made the point by adding the details:

> The way the English Officials handled the 1908 marathon was very controversial since they were obviously biased against an American competitor. For example, officials helped the Italian competitor so that the American wouldn't win.
> The Italian, Pietri, was leading the race, followed at

some distance by an American, Johnny Hayes. Pietri was so exhausted when he entered the stadium for the finish that he turned the wrong way. When he saw his mistake, he did something not uncommon for marathon runners—he collapsed (Paul and Orr 36). In *The Olympic Games,* C. Robert Paul and Jack Orr tell the rest of the story:

> No one else was yet on the stadium track, of course, so little Pietri just lay there for a minute. There were scattered shouts, "Give him a hand, there," "Help him, help him!" Finally, officials illegally lifted him to his feet and began pushing him toward the finish. He fell down three times more, but each time he was helped up. The Italian was standing there in a daze when into the stadium roared the American Johnny Hayes. When the British officials saw yet another American victory in the making, they picked up Pietri and literally dragged him across the finish line. Hayes finished under his own power, thirty seconds later (36–38).

> Clearly, this blatant partisanship did not make the British look like very good hosts for the Olympics.

See the difference details make? The first general version may conjure pictures in the *writer's* mind because the writer had the advantage of doing the research and reading the entire story. But general statements often conjure nothing in the *reader's* mind. As a writer, you need to show the reader the pictures you have seen and wish to communicate.

THE CONCLUSION

The conclusion usually serves two purposes: It summarizes the main points, and it provides a sense of finality (so the reader doesn't turn the last page and expect to find more text).

You may wonder why you need to summarize since you've already made your main points. In a short paper, you probably do not have to summarize. A summary would seem redundant at best, a boring finale at worst. But in a longer paper—even just a few pages—your reader might have gotten so engaged with each main point that he or she would appreciate a reminder of what's gone before. In that case, a summary is useful.

As for providing a sense of finality, you generally want something called a clincher. Clinchers often demonstrate a final flair, like a gymnast finishing with a flourish at the end of a routine. You want to do the same thing, but you don't necessarily have to be flashy. One good clincher is simply a reference to something you used in the introduction, a reminder to the reader that you have now come full circle. And to finish a shorter paper and even some longer ones, just stop.

6

Using Research Material

One of the most important lessons in the research paper process is learning how to present the quotations, paraphrases, and summaries you've worked hard to find. To succeed, you'll have to resist the almost irresistible: the urge to write a paper that *displays* your research material instead of using it for support. Keep in mind that your goal is not to draw attention to good quotations but to use all kinds of research material to persuade your readers to accept your thesis. Yes, you want your readers to notice how good that material is. But you also want your readers to notice that you use it correctly—to reinforce your ideas with convincing support. You want your readers to think, "This is really an interesting, convincing paper," not just, "Looks like some good quotations here and there."

WHEN TO QUOTE

As a general rule, *quote only when you have a good reason to do so.* Use summaries and paraphrases the rest of the time. Beginning writers often reverse this rule, quoting frequently and almost exclusively, probably because paraphrasing and summarizing require an extra step: mentally processing the material and converting it to the writer's own words. But therein lies the value. Because paraphrases and summaries are in the writer's own words, they draw less attention to themselves and interrupt the flow of the paper less. Most of the time they also make for greater economy and sharper focus of supporting evidence. The result is that the readers are more likely to stay with the logic of the paper—the argument being presented—than when they run up against quotation after quotation.

CRITERIA FOR QUOTING

Still, there are good reasons to quote, and properly selected quotations can be the most effective parts of your paper. One good time to quote is when the original material is worded especially well, when not just the content but the style, too, is worth retaining. For example, after describing in detail the first ascent of the Matterhorn and then describing the desolation and anguish of seeing four of his companions fall to their deaths during the descent, Edward Whymper wrote a particularly moving passage:

> Others may tread its summit-snows, but none will ever know the feelings of those who first gazed upon its marvellous panorama; and none, I trust, will ever be compelled to tell of joy turned into grief, and of laughter into mourning. It proved to be a stubborn foe; it resisted long, and gave many a hard blow; it was defeated at last with an ease that none could have anticipated, but, like a relentless enemy—conquered but not crushed—it took terrible vengeance.[1]

Would you want to quote this passage in a paper on mountain climbing? Perhaps. It meets the test of being worded especially well. Now you must consider the relationship of this passage to the paper you are writing. If you're writing about the Matterhorn, this passage might provide a dramatic conclusion to your paper or support an important point you are making. In either case, quoting all or part of this passage could be justified.

Sometimes, too, the exact words are worth retaining because the writer has written very clearly. This can be important when you're trying to express a somewhat complicated process or technique and you know that a paraphrase or summary would be a poor cousin to the original. Suppose, for example, that you're writing about how both patrons and employees of gambling establishments attempt to cheat the house. One part of your paper might deal with the methods patrons use to cheat slot machines and the countermeasures the gambling houses use to prevent that cheating. You might consider quoting all or part of this passage:

> Another lucrative slot scam is called stringing and involves drilling a hole through a silver dollar and tying a string to it. (Dental floss and three-pound monofilament are currently the strings of choice.) Most slot machines are activated by a microswitch located about three inches below the coin drop; to string, you drop your dollar far enough to trigger the switch, then pull it back up. Unlikely as it sounds, lots of people string.
>
> But your average Ike dollar, while passing through the coin acceptor, activates the machine's microswitch for only 20 milliseconds. And

---

[1] Edward Whymper, *Scrambles Amongst the Alps in the Years 1860–69,* 5th ed. (London: Murray, 1900) 393.

even the best stringer on the planet can't drop and retrieve his coin in so short a time. Hence, the coming of the antistring modification, first perfected by an engineer at the downtown Mint casino. When the microswitch remains activated even a twitch longer than 20 milliseconds, the machine automatically locks and sets off an alarm.[2]

This passage does do an unusually good job of explaining ideas that, if not complicated, at least are not particularly simple. Before deciding to quote it, though, you would want to make sure the passage would make a significant contribution to your paper.

Another appropriate time to quote is to take advantage of the words of an authority. The authority doesn't necessarily have to be a famous person, though—just someone in a position to know. For example, *Time* magazine quotes an employee of the Dieppe gambling casino in France as saying, "The croupiers [attendants at gambling tables] could have swiped the chandeliers from the casino if they had wanted to."[3] To support a point about the ease with which employees of gambling houses can cheat management, this passage might deserve the emphasis that quoting would give it.

Finally, another good time for quoting instead of paraphrasing or summarizing is when you are using primary source material. As we explained at the beginning of Chapter 4, a primary source is the origin of basic facts on your subject, whereas a secondary source uses primary sources or other secondary sources as its basis. In writing your own critique of a novel, you'll no doubt want to quote some of the key passages you discuss. You also may want to use some of the critic's views, but summarizing or paraphrasing them often is advisable. You do not always have to quote primary material and always summarize or paraphrase secondary material, of course. You're simply more likely to quote from primary material because more often it will meet the other criteria for quoting: wording that is especially effective or clear or material that is from an authority on the subject.

WHEN NOT TO QUOTE

Now that we've shown some examples of when to quote, let's look more closely at an example of when not to quote—when, in this case, a paraphrase would be more effective.

While she was conducting research for her paper on the early modern Olympics, the writer of the sample paper in Chapter 7 decided to show that the 400-meter race in the 1908 Olympics was controversial. She found this passage:

---

[2] Michael Rogers, "The Electronic Gambler," *Rocky Mountain Magazine* Mar. 1980: 23–24.

[3] "Croupier Capers," *Time* 10 Mar. 1980: 46.

Perhaps the biggest uproar came during the running of the 400-meter final. It involved three American runners—W. C. Robbins of Harvard, J. C. Carpenter of Cornell and J. B. Taylor of New York—and a British favorite, Wyndham Halswelle. The crowd, stirred up by local newspapers which had warned that the Americans might gang up on Halswelle, was tense.

As the race progressed and the four turned into the home stretch, Halswelle was running third behind Robbins and Carpenter. Then Halswelle put on a burst of speed and the three were closely bunched. As Carpenter ran wide to meet the challenge, British officials began yelling, "Foul! Foul!" One of the judges stepped in front of Taylor, who wasn't involved. Another judge cut the tape at the finish line before Carpenter, Robbins and Halswelle came across in that order. The judges then deliberated and declared the race void. They disqualified Carpenter for interference and ruled that the race would have to be rerun the next day.

Now furious American officials stormed out, shouted that they had been robbed and refused to let the U.S. runners compete in the rerun. So on the final day Wyndham Halswelle ran the course all by himself and won a gold medal.[4]

This is written clearly enough and with some liveliness, so it could qualify as a quotation. But there is simply too much irrelevant information—readers have no need to know all those names, which could be confusing. So, having no good reason to quote, she decided to paraphrase. Here is the result:

In the 400-meter final, the British crowd, which had been provoked by the newspapers, was convinced that the Americans would conspire against the local sympathetic favorite to keep him from winning. Indeed, the British runner and three Americans were close to each other near the finish when the British officials suddenly shouted that there had been a foul. One of the officials then blocked an American, keeping him from finishing the race, and another cut the tape before the other Americans could cross the finish. Of course, there was an uproar. The British decided to run the race again the next day, but the Americans refused to participate. The British runner ran alone—nobody cried foul this time—and took home a gold medal (Paul and Orr 35). Clearly, this controversy, which had both the British and Americans fuming, did not improve international relations.

Do you see the advantages of paraphrasing? Not only did she exclude information that would be unimportant to her readers, but by tell-

---

[4] C. Robert Paul and Jack Orr, *The Olympic Games: The Thrills and Drama from Ancient Greece to the Present Day* (New York: Lion, 1968) 35.

ing the story of the race in her own words, she did not distract them with the extra attention that a quotation tends to draw to itself.

Summaries, too, function better than quotations when you're presenting basic facts and opinions from a source and have no real need for the original wording. As we noted in Chapter 4, summaries condense material more than paraphrases do. Had the writer of the paraphrase above chosen to present details about the 400-meter race in a much shorter form, she might have written this:

> In the 400-meter final, British officials interfered in the finish of the race and then demanded that it be run again. When the outraged Americans refused to participate, the British athlete ran alone for the gold (Paul and Orr 35).

As an alternative, perhaps the writer could have quoted only key words from the original here and summarized the rest, like this:

> In the 400-meter final, British officials interfered in the finish of the race and "then deliberated and declared the race void. They . . . ruled that the race would have to be rerun the next day." When the outraged Americans refused to participate, the British athlete "ran the course all by himself and won a gold medal" (Paul and Orr 35).

However, these pieces of quotation do not appear to meet the criteria for quoting. Instead, the writer is forced into awkward wording to fit unimportant pieces of the original into her paragraph. Thus, the quoted material adds nothing but does distract. The straight summary, on the other hand, captures the same facts and ideas and flows more smoothly.

The idea, then, is to quote for effect—when the original is particularly well worded, is particularly clear, or represents an authority, especially an authoritative primary source. At other times, show preference to paraphrases and summaries. They allow you to process material—to simplify and tailor it to your needs.

HOW MUCH TO QUOTE

In addition to quoting too often, beginning writers also tend to quote too much. They will quote an entire paragraph when a sentence or two will do, and they will quote a sentence when a phrase will do. One result is that readers have to read more than is necessary. But more important, the effect of the quotation is diluted by the unnecessary words.

Your task, then, is to take a hard look at a passage you plan to quote and decide just how much you really need to illustrate your point. Let's consider an example. The writer of the sample paper we show you in Chapter 7 wanted to present the thoughts of Baron de Coubertin, the father of the modern Olympics, to show the Baron's intentions in reviving the games. The writer wasn't able to find a primary source with de Coubertin's words, but she did find a secondary source that quoted the Baron. Here's the passage that contained information the writer wanted to use:

> Baron de Coubertin foresaw the meetings of sportsmen of all nations. At a time when politicians were arguing about the merits of Free Trade, the movement of goods without tariffs, he said: "Let us export our oarsmen, our runners, our fencers, into other lands. This is the true Free Trade of the future, and the day it is introduced into Europe the cause of peace will have received a new and strong ally."[5]

Our writer wanted to present de Coubertin's idealistic intentions without the unnecessary reference to Free Trade. The first attempt went like this:

> The Baron's other dream was that this revival would bring peace to the nations of the world. As he expressed it, "the day it [the benefit of the Olympics] is introduced into Europe the cause of peace will have received a new and strong ally" (qtd. in Binfield 23).

The writer has cut away part of the passage from Binfield's book, but to keep the rest she has had to put in brackets an explanation for *it,* since that word doesn't make sense without its original context. This awkward intrusion takes away from the effect of the quotation. The real problem is simple: The writer has juggled her wording to accommodate too large a passage from her source. When she saw how awkward the result was, she adapted the quotation to fit her needs, like this:

> The Baron's other dream was that this revival would being peace to the nations of the world. As he expressed it, the revived Olympics would give peace "a new and strong ally" (qtd. in Binfield 23).

The writer of this research paper condensed the key idea from the original paragraph to five words, disposing of awkward, irrelevant ideas and focusing on the key phrase—the important idea she wanted her readers to see.

HOW TO INTEGRATE QUOTATIONS, PARAPHRASES, AND SUMMARIES

In Chapter 8 we discuss the technical manuscript conventions for presenting research material—spacing, punctuation, and so forth. Here we will concentrate on achieving the two objectives of integrating research

[5] R. D. Binfield, *The Story of the Olympic Games* (London: Oxford UP, 1948) 23.

material into your paper: (1) clearly distinguishing between your words and ideas and those from research sources; and (2) at the same time, blending research material smoothly into your paper.

FRAMING RESEARCH MATERIAL

You can achieve both objectives—distinguishing research material from your writing and at the same time blending it into your writing—by using a box or "frame." Whether you're quoting, paraphrasing, or summarizing, think of enclosing your research material in an imaginary frame—something separating the research material from the rest of the paper.

For a quotation, the frame is simple: The material is framed at the beginning with quotation marks and at the end by quotation marks and a parenthetical reference:

> Thoreau's <u>Walden</u> is famous for its wise sayings, as meaningful today as in the mid-1800s when he wrote them. Take, for example, this comment on materialism: ["I see young men, my townsmen, whose misfortune it is to have inherited farms, houses, barns, cattle, and farming tools; for these are more easily acquired than got rid of" (6).] The materials for nineteenth-century materialism are ones that have

There's no doubt where the borrowing begins and ends, is there? The quotation marks at the beginning and the quotation marks and parenthetical reference at the end clearly frame the borrowed material. We've indicated the frame with brackets—but, of course, you would not use these in your paper.

How do you frame paraphrases and summaries since you don't use quotation marks with them? The parenthetical reference usually marks the end, and you signal the beginning with an introduction such as "Dr. Richard Leakey and Roger Lewin argue in *Origins* . . ." or "The attorney for the case, Gary Reimer, commented wryly that. . . ." There are innumerable possible introductions, so you don't need to be stuck with saying only, "So-and-so said. . . ." Let's look at a sample paraphrase:

---

[6] Henry David Thoreau, *Walden, or Life in The Woods and On the Duty of Civil Disobedience* (New York: Signet-NAL, 1960) 8.

> We think of materialism as burgeoning in the twentieth century, made manifest by shiny automobiles, prefab houses, televisions, and narrow (or is it wide?) lapels and gadgety jewelry. But [Henry David Thoreau, famous for his classic nineteenth-century book <u>Walden</u>, bemoaned the things of his era that were both physical and spiritual baggage to the people he knew (6).] And isn't it true today that the people who strive to collect more and more are all the more burdened by

For this paraphrase, "Henry David Thoreau . . . bemoaned" forms the first part of the frame and the parenthetical reference forms the last part. The reader should have no doubt where the borrowed material is.

WHEN TO FRAME

Do you always need to introduce research material by mentioning the source (author or title)? No, but you must be very careful when you don't. If you mention a fact—such as the number of square miles in Nevada—followed by a parenthetical reference, readers will know what the borrowed material is. Similarly, if you're telling a story, such as the narration of some of the Olympic events in the sample paper in Chapter 7, readers don't need a signal for where the borrowing begins. They will know that the stories of the events couldn't possibly have been created in your mind—that they had to come from somewhere else. And the parenthetical reference at the end of the narrative tells where. The rule, then, is to introduce research material whenever there's a chance that readers may think they're reading your words or ideas if you don't provide the introduction. The parenthetical reference tells them clearly where the borrowing *ends,* but the introduction tells them clearly where it *begins.*

INTRODUCING RESEARCH MATERIAL

An introduction also serves another purpose, one helpful for blending the research material into your writing. It not only says that material came from another source but it identifies that source. And readers are curious about that. They probably don't want to know, in the text of the paper, where and when the material was printed, but they would like to know who said it. That applies to quotations, as well as to paraphrases and summaries. You, too, would probably be distracted by suddenly seeing quotation marks in a paper with no indication of who is quoted:

> In fact, airplanes, trains, ships, and trucks may, in the not-too-distant future, no longer be the primary cargo vessels they are today. "If absolute safety could be guaranteed, the nuclear-powered airship [dirigible] could become the cargo workhorse of the world" (Starchild and Holahan 435). Of course, we may never be able to guarantee that the safety

That quotation is spliced so roughly into the text of the paper that it is bound to be distracting.

See the difference that an introduction makes:

> In fact, airplanes, trains, ships, and trucks may, in the not-too-distant future, no longer be the primary cargo vessels they are today. In a journal called The Futurist, Adam Starchild and James Holahan speculate that "if absolute safety could be guaranteed, the nuclear-powered airship [dirigible] could become the cargo workhorse of the world" (435). Of course, we may never be able to guarantee that the safety

Readers probably don't know who those authors are, and they may never have heard of *The Futurist,* but at least the mystery of the source is solved and they can read further without the uneasiness that a quotation by itself tends to produce.

Finally, there is one more good reason to introduce material. Introductions of some sort almost always are necessary for long quotations. Here the introduction not only prevents mystery about who said it, but also provides a perspective on the quotation. If you have a long quotation—anything over a sentence or so—you want to start the readers off by telling them what point you expect them to understand by reading the quotation. That way as they are reading the quotation, they can constantly relate the material to your point. Here's an example:

> Actually, dirigibles may be particularly important to us in the future because, as Starchild and Holahan point out, the fuel cost is low:
>
> > Because of its buoyancy, the fuel cost of getting and keeping the airship aloft dwindles to almost nothing. Conventional aircraft, not being lighter than air, need considerable thrust to get off the ground. They must employ a powered aerodynamic lift, in contrast to the airship's buoyant aerostatic lift (433-34).

PLAGIARISM

Integrating the material you find in your research into your paper doesn't mean presenting it as if it were your own. As we noted in Chapter 4, that would be plagiarism, a major problem you want to avoid. Plagiarism—a form of dishonesty—is presenting someone else's words or ideas without giving credit for them. You avoid plagiarism by documenting the words and ideas of others when you use them in your writing. Chapters 9 through 12 show you in detail the mechanics of documenting—here we're concerned with properly presenting research material in the text of your paper so you're not accused of wrongdoing.

Here are errors you want to avoid:

- Presenting someone else's idea but not documenting it (so the idea seems to be yours).
- Presenting someone else's words without documenting them (so they seem to be part of your writing).
- Quoting someone else's words—perhaps even documenting them—but failing to use quotation marks (even with parenthetical documentation, readers still will think the words are yours unless you use quotation marks).

If you're careful to keep track of your sources' words and ideas when you take notes and then are careful when you work the material into your paper, you're not likely to be guilty of any of these errors. Conscientiously using the frame when you present research material and using quotation marks when you quote will eliminate the risk of plagiarizing.

However, just for emphasis, let's look more closely at the third item in the list above—it seems to be the most troublesome. Suppose this passage is the source material being used for a paper:

> Combining flexibility and range with enormous payload capacities, giant airships could alter today's whole system of moving materials. Such airships could haul huge loads of the kind that conventional carriers now find economically unfeasible (Starchild and Holahan 435).

Now here's a dishonest use of that passage in a paper:

> There is a good chance that dirigibles could become an important means of transportation. As Starchild and Holahan note, their range and flexibility would be combined with enormous payload capacities, thus perhaps altering our system of moving materials. Dirigibles could carry much more cargo than conventional carriers now find economically feasible (435).

Is there a frame? Yes, there is an introduction at the beginning and a parenthetical reference at the end. The problem is that within the frame are key words from the original—even though the writer appears to be merely paraphrasing. Here's that dishonest passage with the troublesome key words underlined so that you can see the plagiarism:

> There is a good chance that dirigibles could become an important means of transportation. As Starchild and Holahan note, their <u>range and flexibility</u> would be <u>combined with enormous payload capacities</u>, thus perhaps <u>altering</u> our <u>system of moving materials</u>. Dirigibles could carry much more cargo than <u>conventional carriers now find economically feasible</u> (435).

The writer has borrowed key words when he seems to be borrowing only ideas. Without quotation marks, the documentation accounts only for borrowed ideas. The solution is either quotation marks around all the key words (which would be awkward), a less direct rewording (a true paraphrase, in other words), or—probably best of all if the writer really feels he needs every bit of the original material—a quotation.

Use your good judgment and document whenever you are in doubt. Your instructor would prefer too much documentation rather than too little.

EXERCISES

A. Use the following quotation from Charles Darwin's book *The Descent of Man* for items 1 and 2 below.

> The main conclusion arrived at in this work, and now held by many naturalists who are well competent to form a sound judgment, is that man is descended from some less highly organized form. The grounds upon which this conclusion rests will never be shaken, for the close similarity between man and the lower animals in embryonic development, as well as in innumerable points of structure and constitution . . . are facts which cannot be disputed.

1. Either paraphrase this selection or make a combination of paraphrase and key quotations. If you do quote any key phrases, though, be sure to use quotation marks.

2. Now add the "frame" to your paraphrase or combination of paraphrase and key quotations. That is, add a smooth introduction that mentions the author, title, or both; and add this parenthetical reference: (Darwin 3)

B. Use this second quotation from Darwin's *The Descent of Man* for items 1 to 3 below.

> The main conclusion arrived at in this work, namely that man is descended from some lowly-organized form, will, I regret to think, be highly distasteful to many persons. But there can hardly be a doubt that we are descended from

barbarians. The astonishment which I felt on first seeing a party of Fuegians [natives of the South American island Tierra del Fuego] on a wild and broken shore will never be forgotten by me, for the reflection at once rushed into my mind—such were our ancestors. These men were absolutely naked and be-daubed with paint, their long hair was tangled, their mouths frothed with ex-citement, and their expression was wild, startled, and distrustful. They pos-sessed hardly any arts, and like wild animals lived on what they could catch; they had no government, and were merciless to everyone not of their own small tribe.

1. Make a brief summary of the entire passage above.

2. Now add the frame to your summary; use "(Darwin 3)" as the parentheti-cal reference.

3. Assume, now, that you are going to quote the entire passage above as support for the point that Darwin appears to pass a moral judgment on the Fuegians based primarily on their outward characteristics. You learned in this chapter that your introduction to long quotations should help give the readers the proper perspective on the quotation. Write a possible introduction that would accomplish that purpose.

C. If the following selection appeared in a paper, why would it be considered plagiarism (see Exercise A)?

> Darwin pointed out in his famous book The Descent of Man that man is descended from some less highly organized form. He felt that the grounds upon which his conclusion rested would never be shaken (3).

D. In addition to the kind of plagiarism illustrated in Exercise C, what are two other kinds of plagiarism?

7 A Sample Research Paper

Throughout the book, we have been discussing the various key parts of the sample research paper on the early modern Olympics. We think it is an example of especially good college-level writing. At the end of the paper is a brief presentation of its organization. You may wish to review that presentation first so you can see how closely the paper's structure matches the model we discussed in Chapters 4 and 5.

CONTROVERSY IN THE EARLY MODERN OLYMPICS

by

Connie Capone

for

English 111
Professor Harrington
April 23, 1987

|A| Notice the placement of the parenthetical documentation reference in relation to the quotation marks and the final punctuation for the sentence. In addition, the parenthetical reference here illustrates documentation for an "indirect reference"—when the source you use quotes another source. You'll find guidance on this and other parenthetical reference formats in Chapter 9.

|B| A quotation by an authority helps make a point if it's reinforced with a specific example—such as the trouble in the earlier 1972 Olympics.

|C| The end of the introduction is a good place for the thesis statement.

|D| This is a background paragraph, and background paragraphs are always risky because they seem to violate the unity of the paper. Readers have just finished the thesis and are ready to read your support; then you sidetrack them, they think, with something else. However, sometimes—like here—background paragraphs provide a necessary perspective. Readers need to know that the early modern Olympics were primitive; otherwise, the overtness of the

Controversy in the Early Modern Olympics

In 1896, the Baron Pierre de Coubertin of France saw one of his dreams come true—the revival of the Olympics after more than a thousand years. The Baron's other dream was that this revival would help bring peace to the nations of the world. As he expressed it, the revived Olympics would give peace "a new and

A strong ally" (qtd. in Binfield 23). But far from helping to bring peace, the Olympics seem to have been more effective at bringing divisiveness of the worst kind. Before the troubles of 1980 and subsequent games, the most blatant example was the 1972 Olympics held in Munich: eleven Israelis were murdered by Arab terrorists as some sort of international protest (<u>The New York Times</u>, 24 Dec. 1972). And the bickering during the 1976 Montreal Olympics caused the director of the International Olympic Committee, Monique Berlioux of

B France, to comment, "Now everybody is using the Olympics as a political tool" (Yalowitz 16). The Baron's second dream, it seems, has turned into a nightmare. Yet it has always been so, even from the beginning. The early "revived" Olympics may not have been used as a political tool, but they were so tainted by parochialism that

C they caused international bitterness rather than international friendship.

D First, let's place these early games in the context of the more recent games we're familiar with. The early games were not very well known. There was some press coverage, of course, but only a column or two in

hometown refereeing may seem too unusual. This information might have fit in the introduction—a good place for background material—but the introduction was geting too long already.

E   An introduction to a quotation can indicate which source from your Works Cited list you're referring to, as this one does by identifying the 26 July 1936 issue of *The New York Times*. Usually, then, all you would need to give in the parenthetical reference would be the page(s) used. In this case, however, that work as described in Works Cited indicates only *one page*. Therefore, *no* parenthetical reference is required.

F   Notice that the last sentence of the background paragraph reminds the readers of the thesis. They're ready once again to read the support.

G   See the parenthetical reference? Where did the paraphrasing begin? Your obligation to your readers is to be sure they always know where borrowed material begins and ends. No problem here: Clearly the borrowed material begins with the first sentence in the paragraph. In Chapter 6 we mentioned that normally you should begin paraphrases by mentioning the source's author or title. That's not necessary here because the reader knows these facts had to

the sports section, not the media blitz we're used to. The games also didn't occupy a very important place in the host country. As <u>The New York Times</u> pointed out

E in a 26 July 1936 review of the Olympics, "The games of 1900 were held as a sideshow to the Paris Exposition of that same year. . . . Foreign competitors were few and native spectators were scarce." Even worse, the events were held in conditions that would truly embarrass the average junior high school today: The runners didn't have a cinder path, the sprint course was hilly, and the discus occasionally landed in a grove of trees (Kieran and Daley 31). Still, these poorly planned and

F administered games managed to generate, if only on a small scale, international controversy and bitterness.

The 1900 Olympics were scheduled to open on Sunday, July 15. When the Americans arrived in France and learned that the opening was scheduled for the Sabbath, they threatened to boycott the competition. But the French didn't want to start a day early, on July 14, because that was Bastille Day, their most important national holiday. The French feared that nobody would be interested enough to watch the Olympics when they could watch parades and other celebrations instead. And the French were right. They relented, held the opening and first-round events on Bastille Day, and

G hardly anybody showed up (Kieran and Daley 31-34).

Then the intrigue: The French held a secret meeting that excluded the Americans, and scheduled some final round events for Sunday. The Americans were outraged, and many of them refused to compete on that

come from a source other than the writer of the research paper. But if you ever think the reader may have a question about where your borrowed material begins, introduce it by mentioning the author's name or the title of the source.

H   Notice the clear shift from one major section of the paper (the 1900 Olympics) to the other major section (the 1908 Olympics). By the way, such an explicit topic sentence for the section on the 1900 Olympics was not necessary because readers knew they were about to read support. The restated thesis at the end of the background paragraph had just prepared them.

day. The French were more stubborn this time and held the events anyway (Kieran and Daley 33-34). In total, the Americans still managed to win 17 of the 23 track and field events (Paul and Orr 32)—some performers, including some on the second string, had no particular scruples about the Sabbath and won their events (Kieran and Daley 34)—but the bitterness that resulted meant that there were probably no real winners at the 1900 games. There were only losers.

H The 1908 Olympics held in London didn't do much for de Coubertin's "ally" of peace, either. They even started badly—the flags of Sweden and the United States were missing from those displayed at the stadium on opening day; the Finns couldn't carry their flag during the parade because the Russians insisted that the Finns must carry the Russian flag; and the Irish were upset because they had to compete under Great Britain's Union Jack (Kieran and Daley 63-64).

The bitterest controversies, however, involved two races: the 400-meter final and the marathon. In the 400-meter final, the British crowd, which had been pro-voked by the newspapers, was convinced that the Americans would conspire against the local sympathetic favorite to keep him from winning. Indeed, the British runner and three Americans were close to each other near the finish when the British officials suddenly shouted that there had been a foul. One of the officials then blocked an American, keeping him from finishing the race, and another cut the tape before the other Americans could cross the finish. Of course, there was

[I]   Notice the introduction to the long quotation. This introduction does two things. It tells the readers what to look for in the quotation: "the rest of the story." Second, it mentions the source; otherwise, readers would wonder where it came from, and there is no need to send readers to your documentation or, more likely, to leave them vaguely dissatisfied or distracted.

[J]   Why a long quotation from a secondary source? Normally it's not advisable, unless the source says something so well that paraphrasing would be a poor cousin. We think the writer chose well here.

an uproar. The British decided to run the race again the next day, but the Americans refused to participate. The British runner ran alone—nobody cried foul this time—and took home a gold medal (Paul and Orr 35). Clearly, this controversy, which had both the British and Americans fuming, did not improve international relations.

But the most serious controversy was to follow with the marathon, which, perhaps more than any other event, has come to symbolize the Olympics. An Italian, Pietri, was leading the race, followed at some distance by an American, Johnny Hayes. Pietri was so exhausted when he entered the stadium for the finish that he turned the wrong way. When he saw his mistake, he did something not uncommon for marathon runners—he collapsed (Paul and Orr 36). In The Olympic Games, C. Robert Paul and Jack Orr tell the rest of the story:

[I]

[J]

> No one else was yet on the stadium track, of course, so little Pietri just lay there for a minute. There were scattered shouts, "Give him a hand, there," "Help him, help him!" Finally, officials illegally lifted him to his feet and began pushing him toward the finish. He fell down three times more, but each time he was helped up. The Italian was standing there in a daze when into the stadium roared the American Johnny Hayes. When the British officials saw yet another American victory in the making, they picked up Pietri and literally dragged him across the finish line. Hayes finished under his own power, thirty seconds later (36-38).

After arguing for some time, the British officials finally disqualified Pietri, who was still the crowd's choice, and

K   Once again, notice that the introduction to the long quotation mentions the source and tells the reader what to look for in the quotation. And again no parenthetical reference is required because the
source as described in Works Cited indicates only one page.

L   This quotation comes from *The New York Times,* which most college
libraries have on microfilm. *The New York Times* can provide good
primary source material.

M   Notice the square brackets, not parentheses, for the explanatory
comment. The square brackets indicate to the reader that "Pietri"
was not part of the quotation.

N   Notice the ellipsis (see Chapter 8). The spaced periods, positioned
as these are, mean that anything, from the end of a sentence, to
several sentences, to multiple paragraphs, has been deleted. See
Chapter 8 for instructions on altering quotations.

awarded the gold medal to the American (Kieran and Daley 72). Later, the Queen gave Pietri a special award to recognize his performance (Paul and Orr 38).

The American papers reacted strongly against the partisanship of the British officials. The New York Times, in a 7 August 1908 article deploring the situation, quoted one of the American Olympic athletes on his reaction to the marathon dispute:

> I believe if those who had been following this runner around the course had seen that it was a runner from the United Kingdom who was in second place they would have been willing to hit Dorando [Pietri] over the head rather than have him cross the line. But it was an American who was in second place, so they wanted the Italian to win.

The 19 November 1908 Times of London, on the other hand, tended to blame the troubles on the Americans, commenting that many of the American athletes and officials were in fact Irish-Americans who were anti-English.

At any rate, the 1908 Olympics did not do much to improve British-American relations, as The New York Times commented on 26 July 1908:

> Thoughtful men in England have serious doubts, and these doubts are being expressed in some of the most influential newspapers, as to whether the Olympian games serve any good purpose, while theoretically they are supposed to foster international friendship. The result of the meeting just finished has been to create international dissensions and to kindle animosities. . . .
> As a means of promoting international friendship it has been a deplorable failure.

O   The last sentence of the quotation states a nice idea to end the paragraph with, but that ending would have been awkward since the conclusion comes next. Hence, this short sentence.

P   This sentence restates the thesis and summarizes the paper.

Q   Notice the reference to the motivator in the introduction. Many writers use this technique to bring their papers "full circle."

R   The clincher does not create a question that would need another research paper for proof.

6

O   Indeed, the early revived games were not off to a good start.

P   Pettiness and hometown refereeing ultimately overshadowed any good that might have developed from the early modern Olympics. At this stage, the games had not yet been used as a forum for political protest since most of the controversies arose instead from the conduct of the games. But the problems were still seri-

Q   ous enough that instead of becoming de Coubertin's "strong ally" for world peace, the Olympics became just one more enemy. And the Americans and the British, the Americans and the French, were not even at war.

R   Ostensibly, at this time and in the world war soon to come, they were the best of friends.

S   The Works Cited listing begins on a separate page from the body of the research paper. Chapter 10 explains in detail the style for Works Cited entries and for formatting the Works Cited page(s).

7

Works Cited

[S] Binfield, R. D. <u>The Story of the Olympic Games</u>. London:

Oxford UP, 1948.

Kieran, John, and Arthur Daley. <u>The Story of the Olym-</u>

<u>pic Games: 776 B.C.-1968 A.D.</u> Rev. ed. Philadelphia:

Lippincott, 1969.

<u>The New York Times</u> 26 Jul. 1908, sec. 4: 1.

<u>The New York Times</u> 7 Aug. 1908: 6.

<u>The New York Times</u> 26 Jul. 1936, sec. 7: 10.

<u>The New York Times</u> 24 Dec. 1972, sec. 5: 1.

Paul, C. Robert, and Jack Orr. <u>The Olympic Games: The</u>

<u>Thrills and Drama from Ancient Greece to the Pres-</u>

<u>ent Day</u>. New York: Lion, 1968.

<u>Times</u> [London] 19 Nov. 1908: 7.

Yalowitz, Gerson. "Behind the Pageantry and Thrills: No

End of Trouble for Olympics." <u>U.S. News & World Re-</u>

<u>port</u> 2 Aug. 1976: 16-17.

COMMENTS ON ORGANIZATION AND SUPPORT

Did you notice that the organization of the sample paper follows our model quite well?

INTRODUCTION:	Thesis: early modern Olympics produced international bitterness
FIRST MAIN POINT:	background on the primitiveness of the early modern Olympics
SECOND MAIN POINT:	controversies during the 1900 Olympics
THIRD MAIN POINT:	controversies over the 1908 Olympics
CONCLUSION:	includes a summary of thesis and main points

Did you notice the detailed support? We think that the stories of the controversies (and the quotations from the newspapers of the times) give the paper vitality.

If you have any stories to tell in your paper, don't leave them out.

8

The Finished Product: Format Conventions

Once you're satisfied that you have a polished draft of your paper, the next step is to put the paper in final form. To be sure the paper has a professional appearance, you'll want to type it (or have it typed), of course, but there is more to professional appearance than just neatness. You also need to follow certain conventions of format.

A convention is an expected and accepted way of doing something. Conventions of format in writing have to do with aspects of presentation—spacing, margins, and other relative minutiae that usually have little to do with the substance of a paper (what it "says") but that can have a lot to do with a reader's reaction to it (because of "how it looks").

We'll start with special conventions for presenting quotations in the text of your paper and then cover other general conventions that will help you produce a paper with an appearance that does justice to the time you spent writing it.

PRESENTING QUOTATIONS

Be sure you quote accurately. If possible, check the quotations in your final draft against the sources they came from or, if the sources are no longer available or not reasonably handy, against your note cards. You may find you've made mistakes copying quotations from draft to draft.

QUOTING PROSE

Short quotations

If a quotation of prose will take *four or fewer lines of typing* in your paper, it's a *short quotation,* such as the remark by Monique Berlioux in the following excerpt from our paper on the Olympics:

> And the bickering during the 1976 Montreal Olympics caused the director of the International Olympic Committee, Monique Berlioux of France, to comment, "Now everybody is using the Olympics as a political tool" (Yalowitz 16).

You don't have to quote a full sentence if less will do the job. Quote only as much as you need. Here's another excerpt from our paper on the Olympics—this time with only a phrase quoted ("he" below refers to the Baron Pierre de Coubertin):

> As he expressed it, the revived Olympics would give peace "a new and strong ally" (qtd. in Binfield 23).

Whether you quote a full sentence, more, or less, the rules for presenting a short quotation are the same:

- *Type the quotation along with your own writing, without special indentation or spacing.*
- *Use quotation marks to enclose your source's exact words.*
- *Place a parenthetical documentation reference, if required, after the quoted material and before the punctuation mark, if any, that ends the sentence, clause, or phrase with the material it documents.* ("Placement in Text," page 116 in Chapter 9, provides a thorough explanation about placing parenthetical references in the text of your paper.)

Here are the rules for presenting a long quotation of prose in a paper with double-spaced typing:

- *Triple-space before and after the long quotation.*
- *Single-space the quotation itself.*
- *Indent the quotation ten spaces from the left margin but retain the normal right margin.* Indent an extra three spaces from the left for lines that begin paragraphs in the original. That's why the first line of our sample long quotation of prose is indented an extra three spaces.
- *Place a parenthetical reference, if required, after the quoted material and before the punctuation mark that ends the long quotation.* (Our sample has no parenthetical reference because none is required: The introduction to the quotation provides information to identify

the particular source in Works Cited, and no page reference is needed because the source as described in Works Cited has only one page.)

Long quotations

If a prose quotation would take up *more than four lines of typing* in your paper, it's a *long quotation,* and you must give it special treatment so it will be easy to read and clearly identifiable as someone else's words. Here's a long quotation from our paper on the Olympics:

> The American papers reacted strongly against the partisan-
>
> ship of the British officials. The New York Times, in a 7 Au-
>
> gust 1908 article deploring the situation, quoted one of the
>
> American Olympic athletes on his reaction to the marathon
>
> dispute:

> > I believe if those who had been following this run-
> > ner around the course had seen that it was a runner
> > from the United Kingdom who was in second place
> > they would have been willing to hit Dorando [Pietri]
> > over the head rather than have him cross the line. But
> > it was an American who was in second place, so they
> > wanted the Italian to win.

QUOTING POETRY

Presenting quotations of poetry is similar to presenting prose, except there are special rules to account for the existence of defined lines in the poetry. We'll illustrate the rules for presenting quotations of poetry with selections from the following poem:

Resurrection

Slouching grimly from my cold, dark cave,
   I meet my past.
Do I dream, or is the long hibernation
   finally over?

The evening is gentle and pure,
Spring has come at last.

I have walked this path before—
I have seen the stars
   through budding trees,

Closed my eyes
   and felt the breeze
Flowing, gently flowing
   through my hair.

Warmth stirs within me.
The time has come
   once more
To search for you.

Short quotations

Treat a *single line or less of poetry* basically as if it were a short quotation of prose:

> "I have walked this path before" (line 7) means that the narrator feels he has returned to a place in his life where he felt both happiness and hope.

Notice that the quotation is typed along with the student's own writing, without special indentation or spacing, and quotation marks enclose the exact words from the source. The parenthetical reference, however, is different, although the guidance for placement in the text is unchanged. (See "Citing Literary Works" on page 114 of Chapter 9 for a discussion of switching to line citations in your parenthetical references when you quote poetry, as in the sample here. The parenthetical reference—"(line 7)"—assumes that a first full parenthetical reference has already occurred to identify the page reference for the poem as a whole.)

For *two or three lines of poetry,* presentation is similar, except a slash (/) with a space on each side separates the poetic lines:

> The opening lines, "Slouching grimly from my cold, dark cave, / I meet my past," indicate that the narrator is like a bear who has been hibernating, reduced to bodily survival with no passion for life or beauty.

(Notice that no documentation is provided for the line numbers here because the introductory comment—"The opening lines"—is sufficient reference, assuming again that the student already has established that references are to a particular poem.)

Long quotations

Presentation of *more than three lines of poetry* is something like presentation of a long quotation of prose:

> After the narrator emerges from his emotional hibernation, a revived hunger for love and companionship stirs within him, just as the hunger for food and a mate stirs within a bear emerging from the sleep of a long, cold winter:
>
> > Warmth stirs within me.
> > The time has come
> >   once more
> > To search for you (lines 14-17).

The word "you" in the final line is a personification of all that the narrator had set aside during his hibernation but now seeks.

Here are the rules for presenting a long quotation of poetry in a paper with double-spaced typing:

- *Triple-space before and after the quotation.*
- *Indent ten spaces from the left margin.*
- *Single-space the quotation itself.*
- *Double-space between stanzas.*
- *Retain the poetic lines and any other special spacing or punctuation features of the poem.* If you can't fit a whole line of the poem on your typed page, continue on the next line of your page, indenting five extra spaces from the left margin of the poem.
- *Don't use quotation marks unless they appear in the poem.*

ALTERING A QUOTATION

Omitting words

Sometimes you want to omit words from something you're quoting because they're irrelevant or awkward out of their original context. You must ensure that the edited passage fits into the grammar and sense of your own writing. Moreover, if there is any possibility your readers might not otherwise realize a cutting has been made, you owe it to both your source and your readers to make clear that you have altered the passage. The device you use is an ellipsis (. . .)—three spaced periods with a space at the beginning and end.

When you quote only a word or phrase, you don't need to show that material has been left out before and after the quotation—the cutting is clear enough. However, when the editing results in a complete sentence (or a complete line of poetry), you need to use the ellipsis to show that you have modified the original, no matter how minor the change. It is *never* acceptable to edit the original so that you change its meaning; omissions are acceptable only as a convenience to trim unnecessary words or to fit the quotation into the pattern of your writing. But you always must do this editing without damaging the sense of the original. The ellipsis, then, functions as a device for intellectual honesty: It warns readers that you have knowingly edited the quotation, and your readers will assume that you have done so properly. Your readers will also see where to check the original if they have difficulty accepting the way you have used the altered quotation.

When the omission occurs *inside a sentence (or a line of poetry),* the remainder will look like this:

"On the other hand, some . . . were not convinced."

If the omission occurs at the *end of a sentence,* use four spaced periods without a space in front of the first period (that is, you add a sentence period to the ellipsis). The following passage:

> "The Americans were outraged, and many of them refused to compete on that day. The French were more stubborn this time and held the events anyway."

could become this:

> "The Americans were outraged. . . . The French were stub-born this time and held the events anyway."

Notice that there is no space between "outraged" and the first period. If the omission immediately precedes a parenthetical reference, show the ellipsis before the parentheses and the sentence punctuation after:

> "The Americans were outraged . . . " (4).

Notice that this time there is a space between "outraged" and the ellipsis and between the ellipsis and the ending quotation marks.

An ellipsis at the end of a sentence (whether at the end of a quotation or not) can represent omission of the end of the sentence, one sentence, several sentences, a paragraph, or several paragraphs. At the end of a line of poetry, it would indicate omission of one or more lines of poetry.

Adding words

Sometimes you need to add an explanation within a quotation so that the quotation will make sense in the context of your writing. Use square brackets to separate your words from those you're quoting:

> "The day it [the benefit of the Olympics] is introduced into Europe, the cause of peace will have received a new and strong ally."

Don't use parentheses instead of brackets, or your readers may think they're still reading part of the quoted material.

Some typewriters don't have keys for brackets. If yours doesn't, draw in the brackets neatly by hand, using black ink or pencil.

Adding emphasis

You also can highlight or emphasize a portion of a quotation by under-lining (or italicizing) it. However, you must ensure that readers can tell who added the emphasis, you or the original writer. Ordinarily any underlin-ing (or italics) in a quotation belongs to the original passage. Therefore, if you alter the material, provide an explanation at the end of the quotation:

> "And the French were <u>right</u>" (emphasis added).

Notice that the comment is in parentheses rather than square brackets. Comments attached outside a quotation can go into parentheses; those added inside the quotation must go into square brackets.

Verifying quotation accuracy

If you find an error, or material that may seem to be peculiar, in the quotation you want to use, add "sic" to the quotation—in square brackets if inside the quotation and in parentheses if outside. The word *sic* is Latin for "thus." Used with a quotation it is understood to mean, "The wording, spelling, and punctuation were *thus* in the original. I have recorded them faithfully":

> "The Olimpics [sic] caused no end of trouble."

If you quote a passage that itself contains an ellipsis or words in brackets, again use "sic" to verify that you have quoted accurately. Without this warning, readers will assume that an ellipsis or words in brackets in a quotation result from your altering of the passage.

Of course, if you are quoting extensively from material that appears markedly different from what is accepted today—spelling in medieval or Renaissance literature, for example—the irregularities will be accepted as part of the norm. You don't need to mark each instance with "sic."

Altering final punctuation

Within a quotation, punctuation must appear as in the original, unless properly modified through use of an ellipsis (you can delete internal punctuation along with words) or square brackets (you can add punctuation as well as words). Final punctuation, however, will depend on how you integrate the quotation into your own writing. This quotation:

> "The Olympics have always created political problems."

ends with a period, yet you might change that period to a comma if the quotation became an internal clause in your writing:

> "The Olympics have always created political problems," commented columnist Bernard Johnson.

The next section provides guidance for placement of quotation marks in relation to punctuation marks.

PUNCTUATION WITH QUOTATION MARKS

Periods and *commas* always go *inside* quotation marks, even if the mark is part of your sentence and not part of the quotation:

> The columnist said that "the Olympics have not been beneficial to the hosts."

Colons and *semicolons* always go *outside* quotation marks:

> The columnist said that "the Olympics have not been beneficial to the hosts"; unfortunately, many other people agree with him.

Question marks and *exclamation points* go inside the quotation marks if the quotation itself is a question or an exclamation. Otherwise, place them outside the quotation marks:

> The columnist asked, "Do you really believe that the Olympics have been beneficial to the hosts?"

> Did the columnist say that "the Olympics have not been beneficial to the hosts"?

> Why did the columnist ask, "Do you really believe that the Olympics have been beneficial to the host?"

(In the final example above, both the textual sentence and the quotation are questions.)

OTHER FORMAT CONVENTIONS

The rest of this chapter provides recommendations for a number of those minutiae you need to know about in preparing the final version of your research paper. The rules aren't absolute, of course, and your instructor may want to modify some of them.

TYPING/WORD PROCESSING

Whether you actually type your paper or use a computer (the preferred method by far), be sure that your final product is easy to read. Your typewriter should have clean keys. A letter "e" with the hole filled in won't make a very good impression. Your typewriter (or computer printer) should also have a good ribbon.

Most instructors are glad to accept dot matrix printing, but you might check with your instructor first, just to be sure.

Should you use a typewriter or a word processor (computer)? The answer is easy: If you have access to a word processor, by all means, use it. It has several overwhelming advantages over the typewriter:

1. You can make corrections easily. That means you're far more likely to engage seriously in the revising process.
2. You can, with many programs, use a spelling checker. That means you'll not only correct words you've misspelled but correct typos, too. By helping with the technicalities, the word processor frees you to think more about the larger, more important matters of writing. You must be careful, though, because spelling programs can't pick up all errors.
3. Most important from our point of view, the word processor helps you get words on paper more easily in the first place—especially if you can compose at the keyboard. Anybody who has tried this method knows it is the primary benefit of the word processor, and they often refuse to write any other way.

PAPER

Use white 8½- × 11-inch typing paper. Many instructors prefer the "erasable" paper because it's easy for students to correct. But because it smudges easily and is hard to write comments on, other instructors prefer that you use a reasonably heavy bond paper. Avoid thin "onion skin" paper because it's flimsy to hold and also is hard for your instructor to write on.

COVER SHEET

The cover sheet, if you use one, should give at least the title of your paper and your name. Most instructors also want the course number, instructor's name, and date the paper is submitted. The sample paper in Chapter 7 shows a format you can use; the technical paper in Chapter 14 uses a similar format. Some instructors do not require a title page, preferring instead that the information be given on the first page of text.

MARGINS AND SPACING

All margins should be one inch. However, if you submit the paper in a folder or binder, make the left margin 1½ inches. Indent an extra five spaces from the left to start paragraphs. Double-space when you type, except for special-format items as identified earlier in this chapter and in Chapter 11.

NUMBERING PAGES

Use Arabic numerals (2, 3, 4, and so on) and place the number in the top, right corner of the page ½ inch from the top of the page and in line with the right margin. Don't number the first page of your text, but do count it as page 1. If you have preliminary matter (such as an outline, a table of contents, or a preface), use small Roman numerals (i, ii, iii, and so on). Center the small Roman numerals beneath the bottom margin of each preliminary page.

HEADINGS

Headings are handy. We use them often in this book and you should consider using them, too. We cover them in Chapter 14 because they're almost obligatory for technical papers.

FASTENING THE PAPER

We recommend that you staple the paper in the upper left corner. Many instructors don't like paper clips because they tend to come off or fasten onto other papers. Other instructors prefer paper clips. Some instructors will allow (or require) you to put your paper in a plastic folder or binder, but many instructors consider folders a bother when they try to review your work.

CORRECTIONS

Try not to have any obvious corrections. But if you catch an error at the last minute, correct it neatly with black ink or pencil. After all, neatly typed errors probably won't do you much good.

DOCUMENTATION

The next four chapters cover documentation styles. Chapter 9 explains *parenthetical documentation;* you'll use it along with Chapter 10, Works Cited. However, if your instructor requires you to use *documentation with notes* instead, we cover that style in Chapter 11. Chapter 12 covers other documentation styles.

9

Parenthetical
Documentation

In this chapter, as well as the two that follow it, you'll learn about another kind of convention for format in a research paper. Here, though, rather than conventions for presenting research material in the body of your paper or for the layout of the paper as a whole (the topics of the last chapter), you'll learn about the special format conventions for documenting the sources of the research information you incorporate into the text of your research paper. Whether you present that information as quotations, paraphrases, or summaries, you must document the sources of the information. As with other aspects of presentation, there are accepted (hence, expected) styles for showing documentation. Understanding how you are expected to document is one of the major learning experiences of studying how to write a research paper.

The formats for documentation in this chapter, as well as Chapters 10 and 11, generally follow the second edition of the *MLA Handbook for Writers of Research Papers,* published by the Modern Language Association. This handbook is an accepted standard for documentation style in many academic fields, especially the humanities. There are other style guides, of course, and there are differences from one guide to another on specific entry and page formats. We've chosen to follow MLA on most points because the guidance is thorough, reasonable, and widely accepted.

Don't be too concerned about differences among style manuals. Most differences exist to accommodate the varied needs of differing academic fields. More important, however, most documentation guides differ little on what should go into a specific documentation entry for an article or book. In practical terms, then, if you learn one system well, you can adapt easily to the particular conventions required in another place at another time. You'll know basically what should be in documentation entries by anybody's standard, so you'll be able to see quickly the peculiarities of another system. Thus, when you've practiced documentation in the style shown here, you'll have in hand one good, general-purpose documentation system.

This chapter teaches use of *parenthetical documentation* in the text of your research paper, establishing simple references to a Works Cited list (the subject of Chapter 10) at the end of the paper. A more traditional style of reference uses footnote or endnote reference numbers in the text of the paper with reference information at the bottom of each page or at the end of the research paper. Because some instructors prefer this style of *documentation with notes,* we've explained the format conventions for that style in Chapter 11. If you have no interest in parenthetical documentation but want to learn about documentation with footnotes or endnotes, skip the rest of this chapter, read Chapter 11, and then read Chapter 10. Chapter 12 covers two more documentation styles—the *APA system* and the *numbered reference system*—styles particularly appropriate for some of the social and physical sciences. For these, skip to Chapter 12 and then read Chapter 10.

PARENTHETICAL DOCUMENTATION SYSTEM

The parenthetical documentation system depends on the interaction of material you place in two portions of your research paper:

- *General source listing.* At the end of your research paper you provide an alphabetized listing, usually called Works Cited, of entries with full bibliographic information about each source document for your research paper. The list provides a general reference to your sources but, of course, does not identify the specific portions you used for the quotations, paraphrases, and summaries in the body of the paper.

- *Specific portion reference.* Within the body of your paper, along with each presentation of material from your sources, you include in parentheses a documentation reference to the specific portion(s) of the source or sources supporting your text. This parenthetical information provides a reference to the data in the Works Cited listing so that readers can connect the general and specific documentation portions.

When readers combine the information in parentheses in the body of your paper with the full bibliographic information in your Works Cited listing, they have the data they need to locate each source and to find the specific portion you used.

Here's a piece of text from the body of the sample research paper you saw in Chapter 7:

> And the bickering during the 1976 Montreal Olympics
> caused the director of the International Olympic Committee,
> Monique Berlioux of France, to comment, "Now everybody is
> using the Olympics as a political tool" (Yalowitz 16).

The *specific portion reference* is *(Yalowitz 16)*. *Yalowitz* tells readers to look for that entry in the Works Cited listing. At the end of the sample research paper is the *general source listing,* in this case a Works Cited page with nine entries. The last of them is this:

> Yalowitz, Gerson. "Behind the Pageantry and Thrills: No End
> of Trouble for Olympics." U.S. News & World Report 2 Aug.
> 1976: 16-17.

The *16–17* in the Works Cited entry indicates that the Yalowitz article appears on those two pages of the 2 August 1976 issue of *U.S. News & World Report.* The *16* in the parenthetical reference in the text of the paper indicates that the quoted material appears on that page of the article.

Clearly, then, you need to learn the conventions for both the general source and specific reference portions of the parenthetical documentation system. The next chapter focuses on format conventions for the Works Cited listing (the general source portion of parenthetical documentation). The rest of this chapter treats the specific portion references that give the system its name: the parenthetical references.

PARENTHETICAL REFERENCES

BASIC CONTENT

Parenthetical references in the text of your paper should provide your readers with the following information:

- *A reference to the opening of the corresponding entry in the Works Cited list.* If the Works Cited entry shows only one author, the parenthetical reference use that author's last name. The reference also could show two or three last names, one person's name with "et al.," the name of a group, a shortened version of the title, or a name with the title, depending in every case on what information is necessary to identify clearly the *one* work in Works Cited that you are referring to. ("Basic Forms" below details the various possibilities.)

- *Identification of the location within that work of the material you are documenting.* Normally this will be a reference to a single page or several pages. However, when your Works Cited listing shows a multivolume work, the parenthetical reference usually will require a volume number as well as the page(s). In addition, if the reference is to a one-page article, to an article in an encyclopedia that alphabetizes its articles, or to a source that has no pagination (such as a film or videocassette), you will not need to provide a place reference.

BASIC FORMS

The material required for a parenthetical reference varies somewhat with the nature of the work to which you refer from your Works Cited list and with how much of it you cite. (For rules on showing inclusive page numbers, see pages 142–143.)

Work with one name listed

When the Works Cited entry begins with only one person's name, use the last name and the page reference: (Madden 33) or (Madden 33–34). Even if the name has a qualifier such as "ed." or "trans.," you still use only the last name in the parenthetical reference.

Work with two or three names listed

If the Works Cited entry opens with more than one name, so must the parenthetical reference: (Schlagel and Dyer 56) or (Rucker, Dean, and Monet 93).

Work with one name and "et al."

If the Works Cited entry begins with a name and "et al.," which means "and others," include the "et al." in your parenthetical reference: (Novinski et al. 323–24).

Work with group as author

Treat the group just like another author: (National Commission on Aging 576). A reference such as this, of course, could easily interrupt a reader's train of thought; we'll discuss later how to avoid that problem by streamlining parenthetical references.

Work listed by title

If a Works Cited entry begins with the title, then a parenthetical reference to it must use the title, or a reasonable shortened version of it. Be careful in shortening the title, though; make sure to include the word that determines the placement of the entry in your alphabetized Works

Cited listing. For example, a parenthetical reference to a magazine article entitled "A Guide for Beginners in Choosing and Buying a Personal Computer" should not show "Choosing a Personal Computer" as the shortened title. Placement of the entry in Works Cited would be determined by "Guide" rather than by "Choosing." Therefore, "Guide to Choosing a Personal Computer" would be an acceptable shortening. As with other long parenthetical references, streamlining the reference may be worth considering.

Multivolume work

In a reference to a multivolume work, normally you'll give a volume number with the page reference: (Picollo 2:152–53). This is a reference to pages 152–53 of volume 2 of a multivolume work alphabetized in Works Cited under Picollo. However, if the entry in Works Cited clearly identifies only a single volume of the multivolume work, then the parenthetical reference does not need the volume number.

Multiple works listed for the same name(s)

When two or more works are alphabetized in Works Cited for the same name(s), the parenthetical reference must include the title, or a reasonable shortened version of it, of the specific work to which you are referring. If two books are listed for Maria Brewer, then a reference to one of them would look like this: (Brewer, *Aboriginals in Australian Fiction* 64). This is another candidate for streamlining.

Citing an entire work

If you need to document a textual reference to an entire work, then a page reference is inappropriate; the parentheses would contain only the "author" element: (Yalowitz). Streamlining, however, will eliminate the need for any parenthetical reference.

Indirect reference

Although you should attempt to find the original source for a quotation, you may need to quote informaton from a source that quotes the original. If you quote or paraphrase a quotation, add "qtd. in" (for "quoted in") to the parenthetical reference. The first parenthetical reference in the sample research paper shows this type of reference:

> In 1896, the Baron Pierre de Coubertin of France saw one of
> his dreams come true—the revival of the Olympics after
> more than a thousand years. The Baron's other dream was

that this revival would help bring peace to the nations of the world. As he expressed it, the revived Olympics would give peace "a new and strong ally" (qtd. in Binfield 23).

Notice that the context of the quotation clearly identifies who is being quoted.

Multiple works in a reference

To include two or more works in a single parenthetical reference, list each as you would for itself and then use semicolons to connect them: (Garrett 69–72; Taylor 23). Again, streamlining may help reduce the interruption, but if you need to show a long, disruptive list, consider using an actual footnote instead (see the section below on "Notes with Parenthetical Documentation").

Citing literary works

If you are documenting references to passages from literary works available in several editions, it will help readers if you amplify the page reference for the edition you used with extra information to identify where the passage would occur in all editions—for example, chapter (ch.) or book (bk.) for prose; act or scene (sc.) for drama or poetry. To show this amplification in a parenthetical reference, give the page reference for your source, type a semicolon, and then give the extra information: (Schlagel 115; ch. 6) or (115; ch. 6).

For classic plays in verse (such as a Greek drama or a play by Shakespeare) don't give page references at all. Instead, give the number(s) for the major division(s) and the line number(s) with periods separating the numbers: for example, (*Hamlet* 1.5.166–67) would document act 1, scene 5, lines 166 and 167 of Shakespeare's *Hamlet*, as would (1.5.166–67) if we already had established—perhaps in the introduction to a quotation—that we were documenting that particular play.

Similarly, for poetry with major divisions, again you can omit page references and instead give division(s), including lines, separated by periods: (1.1.1.1–4) would indicate book 1, canto 1, stanza 1, lines 1 through 4 of Edmund Spenser's *Faerie Queene* if we had established earlier that we were referring to that particular poem.

This type of citation won't work, of course, for shorter poems that have no divisions other than the lines themselves. Don't use the standard abbreviations for "line" or "lines," since "l." and "ll." are too easy to confuse with numbers; use the words instead. For a single reference to a short poem, give the page number for your source, a semicolon, and the line number(s): (Dorman 56; lines 3–4) or (56; lines 3–4). If in your text you have need to document the same poem a number of times, give a full parenthetical reference for the first occurrence, and thereafter give only lines.

STREAMLINING PARENTHETICAL REFERENCES

Several times we've mentioned the possibility of streamlining. The idea is to keep the information in the parentheses as short as possible so that readers are not distracted. You accomplish this by including part or all of the needed reference in the introduction to the source material you're presenting. If the introduction contains the name of a book's author, then the parentheses might need only the page reference:

> Paula Madden notes the ease with which homemakers can adapt simple file software, or even the more complex relational data base programs, to applications such as indexing home libraries, record collections, greeting card mailing lists, or favorite recipes from dozens of cookbooks (33).

Because "Madden" appears in the introduction to the material from Paula Madden's magazine article, the parenthetical reference is streamlined from (Madden 33) to just (33).

The savings in that instance isn't much, of course, but clearly you can reduce the interruption of the parenthetical reference when several works by the same author appear in your Works Cited list. Without streamlining, a reference might look like this:

> To the skeptic who says that a recipe index on a personal computer is nothing more than a very expensive centralization of the indexes of the individual cookbooks, we can argue that the computer recipe file can be expanded to provide additional information that would be impractical in a cookbook's index. With the addition of a field for "Essential Ingredients," the centralized recipe index then can be used as an aid in deciding what to cook, for instance, when the freezer contains only ground beef and the family is complaining about five nights of hamburgers. A field for "Preparation Time" allows time available before dinner to become a factor in recipe selection. Fields for difficulty of preparation, how well certain family members like the recipe, and so forth, provide flexibility no cookbook index will ever be able to offer (Zimmerman, Using the Personal Computer at Home 117).

The version below streamlines the long parenthetical reference by including most of the required information in the introduction to the summary:

> To the skeptic who says that a recipe index on a personal computer is nothing more than a very expensive centraliza-

tion of the indexes of the individual cookbooks, Eric Zimmerman, in <u>Using the Personal Computer at Home</u>, argues that the computer recipe file can be expanded to provide additional information that would be impractical in a cookbook's index. With the addition of a field for "Essential Ingredients," the centralized recipe index then can be used as an aid in deciding what to cook, for instance, when the freezer contains only ground beef and the family is complaining about five nights of hamburgers. A field for "Preparation Time" allows time available before dinner to become a factor in recipe selection. Fields for difficulty of preparation, how well certain family members like the recipe, and so forth, provide flexibility no cookbook index will ever be able to offer (117).

Keep in mind that streamlining doesn't permit omission of required data about a source, but it can reduce the interruption of the parenthetical references. As you learned in Chapter 6, introducing research material blends the material smoothly into your writing. Streamlining of parenthetical references, then, simply uses the introduction—which has a purpose of its own—to incorporate information that otherwise would have to be included at the end of the presentation.

PLACEMENT IN TEXT

Place the parenthetical references in the text of your paper so that they interrupt the flow of thought as little as possible. Put the parentheses as close as reasonably possible after the end of the material you're documenting, but *always* at the end of a clause or phrase so the reference doesn't intrude. Normally, the parenthetical reference can wait for the end of a sentence. Even with quotations the reference doesn't have to come *immediately* after the quotation marks:

> Jeffrey Palin asserts that "keeping up with the Joneses has become electronic," with personal computers and electronic games becoming the status symbols of the American home (163).

Of course, don't delay the parenthetical reference until the end of a sentence if readers would become confused about what material the reference documents:

> Although Palin insists that "keeping up with the Joneses has become electronic" (163), his position does not account for the many unique applications of the personal computer to the activities of the homemaker.

The reference here is in the middle of the sentence because only the first portion is attributable to the source. Note, however, that the parentheses do come at the end of a clause so the reference intrudes as little as possible.

Notice that the parenthetical reference in the first of the two samples above preceded the period at the end of the sentence, and the parentheses in the second sample came before the comma that ended the clause in which the reference appeared. Always place your parenthetical reference before the punctuation mark, if any, that ends the sentence, clause, or phrase with the material you're documenting. If a quotation ends the sentence, clause, or phrase, place the parenthetical reference between the ending quotation marks and the punctuation for the sentence, clause, or phrase, as in the second sample on the facing page. The following example shows a more common case in which a quotation ends a sentence; the rule for placement of the parentheses relative to the quotation marks and punctuation for the sentence is, of course, the same:

> Because of the number of personal computers and expensive electronic games in American homes, social critic Jeffrey Palin has commented that "keeping up with the Joneses has become electronic" (163).

NOTES WITH PARENTHETICAL DOCUMENTATION

Parenthetical references will take care of almost all documentation references, but they won't accommodate digressions from the text. Avoid long side arguments, but if you must add notes to support your text, use standard footnote or endnote entries: that is, use parenthetical references for your normal documentation, but also use notes for the explanatory digressions, like this one:

> [1]Sloane agrees with Palin that most purchasers of personal computers have not determined how they will use the computer before they buy it (73). See also Webb 15; Martin 227-28; and Roy 7.

Chapter 11 illustrates how to place note numbers in the text and shows formats for footnotes and endnotes.

EXERCISES

A. Given the Works Cited entries below as the general source listing for a research paper, write parenthetical references to show the specific portion references required for the numbered exercise items that follow the list. (Just show the parentheses and what would go in them; don't be concerned for this exercise with placing the references into textual passages.)

Adams, Gayle, and Terri Beals. Aztec Funereal Art. Austin: U of Texas P, 1983.

Brennan, James. "The Solitude of Gabriel Garcia Marquez." Studies in Latin American Fiction 8 (1984): 316-136.

Cross, Amanda, trans. "Rio" and Other Poems. By Vicente Martinez. New York: Shirlington, 1985.

Garrett, Thomas. Pottery and Decorations of the Mimbres. 2 vols. Arlington: Burning Tree, 1985.

Stein, Warren. Art of the Ancient Peoples of Latin America. Albuquerque: La Madera, 1984.

1. Page 53 of *Art of the Ancient Peoples of Latin America.*

2. Page 53 of *Art of the Ancient Peoples of Latin America* if another source by Warren Stein appeared in the same Works Cited listing.

3. Page 36 of the Amanda Cross translation of *"Rio" and Other Poems.*

4. Page 117 of *Aztec Funereal Art.*

5. Page 41 of volume 1 of *Pottery and Decorations of the Mimbres.*

6. Page 321 of "The Solitude of Gabriel Garcia Marquez."

7. A quotation from Scott Rice's *The Fiction of Gabriel Garcia Marquez* that is quoted on page 317 of James Brennan's "The Solitude of Gabriel Garcia Marquez."

B. Rewrite the following passages to streamline their parenthetical references. In your rewritten versions, be sure to modify the material inside the parentheses to account for the information you incorporate into the introduction to the research material. And be sure you've followed the rules for punctuation relative to the parenthetical reference and quotation marks.

1. As one reviewer of software has written, "That famous old lady with the shoe house wouldn't have been so confused if she had used a personal computer and a file program to organize the health, school, and schedule information for each of her many children" (Byrd, "Getting Organized with a PC" 97).

2. It may be true that "Mother Hubbard's cupboard need not have been bare if she had managed her household inventories with a home computer" (Daniels, *Household Management and the Personal Computer* 34), yet she still might have had trouble stocking bones for her dog while she tried to pay for a computer and the software to run it.

10 Works Cited

As you saw in Chapter 9, parenthetical references in the body of your research paper are possible because they refer to a *general source listing* at the end of the paper. This chapter focuses on that source listing—first on the format of the pages for the list as a whole, then on the formats of the entries that appear in the list, and finally on a few special format rules that affect the appearance of parts of some entries.

WORKS CITED PAGE FORMAT

The usual name for the general source listing is *Works Cited*. This title assumes that the listing contains all the works you cite in the body of your paper, yet does not include others that you read but that did not contribute to the ideas or data in your paper. Your instructor might ask you to include the other works you read during research, in which case you could change the title of the general source listing to *Works Consulted*.

For the Works Cited page(s)—or whatever title you give the general source listing—start the list on a new page, numbering that page in sequence with the rest of your paper. Here's how the page should look:

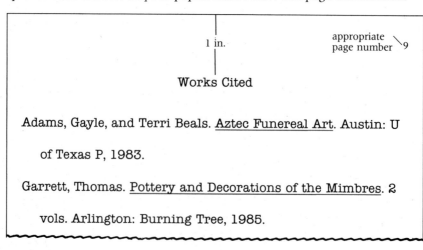

1 in.   appropriate
                                                         page number   9

Works Cited

Adams, Gayle, and Terri Beals. <u>Aztec Funereal Art</u>. Austin: U

    of Texas P, 1983.

Garrett, Thomas. <u>Pottery and Decorations of the Mimbres</u>. 2

    vols. Arlington: Burning Tree, 1985.

- *Use the same margins as for the rest of the pages of your research paper.*
- *Center the title one inch from the top of the page.*
- *Double-space twice after the title to find the line on which to begin the first entry.*
- *Double-space both within and between entries.* (Note: Your instructor may prefer you to single-space within individual entries and double-space only between entries.)
- *Begin the first line of each entry on the left margin, but indent all subsequent lines for an entry five spaces.*
- *List entries in alphabetical order.*

WHAT WORKS CITED ENTRIES CONTAIN

It's commonplace to say that Works Cited entries contain three basic parts: author, title, and publication information. That's true enough for the most simple entries, which normally make up the majority of entries in a list of works cited in a student's paper. However, there are dozens of exceptions to that basic three-part pattern. We believe the following five basic groups more accurately describe a documentation entry and will better help you understand the information you need to record about the sources for your research paper:

1. Person(s) or group responsible for the piece of material you're documenting.
2. The title(s).
3. Amplifying information, to help identify or describe the work precisely.
4. Publishing information, or similar information that will help someone find the work.
5. Identification of the portion you are citing.

Here are those groups in both simple and complex citations:

```
   1                          2                        4
Stein, Warren. Art of the Ancient Peoples of Latin America. Albuquerque: La

Madera, 1984.
```

This example shows one of those simple three-part citations that equate to "author, title, and publication information." Group 3 is missing because no amplifying information is necessary to describe the book, and Group 5 is unnecessary because the entry is for the entire book, not a specific portion of it. An entry for an essay in a collection of essays, however, might have all five basic groups, as this one does:

<pre>
        1   2
Harrison, Adrian N. "Embroidered Figures on Inca Textiles." Art of the Incas. Ed.
        3   4   5
    Clifford Alt. 3rd ed. Austin: U of Texas P, 1985. 176–98.
</pre>

Works Cited entries can be even more complex than this one. Yet despite complexities, the information required falls into the five basic groups.

ENTRIES FOR BOOKS

GENERAL FORM: BOOKS

Divided here into the five basic groups are the thirteen elements you may need for a book citation. Few entries ever actually require all thirteen; the sample simple citation in the previous section, for example, has only five elements, while the sample complex citation has nine. Obviously, you include only those elements that are appropriate for the book (or portion of it) that you're documenting.

Group 1: Person(s) or group responsible for the piece of material you're documenting

- *Name(s) of individual(s) or group.* Usually this is an author, but it can be an editor, translator, or organization. The key is identifying the people *directly responsible* for the particular piece of material you're documenting. Use names as they appear on the title page of the book whenever possible. If the Works Cited entry is to begin with a person's name, reverse the name for alphabetizing (last-first-middle instead of first-middle-last).

Group 2: The title(s)

- *Title of a part of a book.* You'll need this when you're documenting an essay, a poem, a short story, and so forth, within an anthology, or when you cite a division of a book (such as the Introduction).
- *Title of the book.* If a book has both a title and a subtitle, give both with a colon and a single space between them (omitting the colon if the title itself ends with punctuation, such as with a question mark). Special rules beginning on page 140 give guidance for capitalization, quotation marks, and underlining in titles.

Group 3: Amplifying information, to help identify or describe the work precisely

- *Translator(s).* One translation is rarely like another, so it's necessary to show the translator(s) of the work you used.

- *Editor(s).*

- *Edition.* Readers will assume you're citing the first edition, without revisions, unless you indicate otherwise. Portions of different editions of the same book will be different, so you need to show exactly which one you used.

- *Number of volumes.* An indication of the number of volumes in a multivolume set will appear before the publication information; in addition, a volume number also can appear with the page reference, depending on how you refer to the material.

- *Series.* If the work you're citing is part of a series, give the series name and the number of the work in the series (e.g., Studies in Anthropology, No. 7).

Group 4: Publishing information, or similar information that will help someone find the work

- *Publication information: Place.* Look for the place of publication on the title or copyright page, or at the back of the book, especially for a book published outside the United States. If several cities are listed, use the one listed first unless you have some reason for using a different one. Give the state or country if the city is not likely to be recognized or could be confused with another city of the same name.

- *Publication information: Publisher.* You need not name the publisher for a book printed prior to 1900. For books printed since 1900, use a shortened version of the publisher's name, e.g., "Holt" rather than "Holt, Rinehart and Winston." See page 142 for special rules on dealing with publishers' names and special imprints.

- *Publication information: Date.* Again, look for the publication date on the title page, copyright page, or at the back of the book. If no publication date appears, give the latest copyright date. Ignore dates for multiple printings; however, if you are citing a work in other than its first edition, use the publication date for the edition you're using, not the original date. For example, if a book in its third edition shows dates of 1978, 1982, and 1985, use 1985.

Group 5: Identification of the portion you are citing

You'll use this part of an entry only when you're citing a part of a book, such as an essay or an Introduction.

- *Volume number.* For a multivolume work, the volume indication may appear with the page number, depending on how you're referring to the material.

- *Page numbers.* Show the *inclusive* page numbers for the portion of the book you're citing. Don't be concerned if you refer to only one or a few of those pages in the text of your paper; those specific page references will be clear in the parenthetical references in the body of the research paper. Here you must show the pagination for the entire piece. See pages 142–143 for special rules on showing inclusive page numbers.

SAMPLE ENTRIES: BOOKS

Below are samples that illustrate recommended formats for citations of books. A word of caution: A list of samples with an entry to match exactly any book you could find would be incredibly long. The following samples were designed to illustrate particular portions of book citations instead. Therefore, if the book you're citing doesn't quite fit a sample, adapt the format to suit your needs; just be sure to include all the appropriate information you've just read about in the preceding section. Also, because the samples below have been listed to demonstrate points about formats, no attempt has been made to alphabetize them, except for the entries under "Two or More Books by the Same 'Author(s).' " In your Works Cited pages, of course, you'll list works in alphabetical order.

One author

Stein, Warren. <u>Art of the Ancient Peoples of Latin America</u>.
    Albuquerque: La Madera, 1984.

Two or three authors

Only the name of the person listed first is given out of normal order (last-first-middle rather than first-middle-last). Be sure to use authors' names as they appear on the book's title page, including listing them in the order in which they appear (names of multiple authors frequently are not alphabetized on a book's title page).

Adams, Gayle, and Terri Beals. <u>Aztec Funereal Art</u>. Austin: U
    of Texas P, 1983.

Mills, Bruce, Frank J. Jensen, and Larry S. Wilson, Jr. <u>Gemstones and Medieval Medicinal Magic</u>. New York: Schocken, 1985.

More than three authors

For more than three authors, give only the one listed first in the book and follow that with "et al." (for "and others").

Kendall, Melissa, et al. <u>The Amber Wars and the Development of Europe</u>. New York: Shirlington, 1984.

Group as author

If a group or agency is responsible for a book, treat that group as the author and list its name first, even though the group's name may appear in the book's title or as the publisher. ("GPO" in the entry below is the accepted abbreviation for "Government Printing Office," which prints U.S. federal publications.)

National Commission on Aging. <u>Report of the National Commission on Aging</u>. Washington: GPO, 1982.

Government and international body publications

Many government agency publications are simple enough to be treated as books with groups as authors, with the responsible agency serving as author, as in the sample entry above. Occasionally, government publications show a specific person as author; you can begin with that person or show the individual author after the title—the first two samples on the following page illustrate both styles.

For the *Congressional Record*, show only the full date and the inclusive pages for the portion being cited. For other congressional documents, give the government and body, house, committee (if appropriate), document title, number and session of Congress, and type and number of publication, followed by standard publication information. Congressional documents include bills (S 16; HR 63), resolutions (S. Res. 16; H. Res 63), reports (S. Rept. 16; H. Rept. 63), and documents (S. Doc. 16; H. Doc. 63).

There are also documents of state and local governments, foreign governments, and international bodies (such as the United Nations). Begin these as you would a U.S. federal publication, naming first the government or international body (e.g., "Indiana. Dept. of Transportation." or "United Nations. Committee for Economic Cooperation.").

United States. Dept. of State. <u>Islamic Organizations and Stability in the Middle East</u>. By Shirley Fitzsimmons. Washington: GPO, 1985.

Fitzsimmons, Shirley. <u>Islamic Organizations and Stability in the Middle East</u>. U.S. Dept. of State. Washington: GPO, 1985.

<u>Cong. Rec.</u> 8 May 1979: 2756-57.

United States. Cong. House. Permanent Select Committee on Intelligence. <u>Technological Transfer Losses in the 1970s</u>. 102nd Cong., 2nd sess. H. Rept. 1122. Washington: GPO, 1983.

United Nations. Committee for Economic Cooperation. <u>Mineral Development in Southern Africa</u>. Elmsford: Pergamon, 1984.

Author not given

If no author is given in a book, begin the entry with the title. (When you alphabetize the entries for your Works Cited pages, you'll go by the first word in the title other than an article—that is, other than *A, An,* or *The.*) Of course, treat books with groups as authors or government and international body publications as indicated above, even though these books frequently show no individual as author.

<u>A Treasury of Russian Humor</u>. Washington: Luke, 1984.

Editor

If your use of an edited book, for the most part, is the text of the work itself, then the name(s) of the editor(s) (ed. or eds.) should appear after the title, as in the first sample below. However, if the work of the editor(s)—including introductory or other extratextual comments—is being cited, begin the entry with the editor(s), as in the second sample. In addition, if you are citing an anthology or other collection—rather than a piece within the collection—use the second format below (for a piece in a collection, see "Part of a Collection").

Smith, Emily. <u>English Stoneware</u>. Ed. Brooke Harter. Huntington, SC: Hurley Museum, 1981.

Harter, Brooke, ed. <u>English Stoneware</u>. By Emily Smith. Huntington, SC: Hurley Museum, 1981.

Translator

Normally you'll show the translator(s) of a book after the title, as in the first sample below. However, as with editors, if you are citing primarily commentary by the translator(s), then begin with the translator(s), as in the second sample. If the book has both a translator and an editor, show the translator first, as in the third sample.

> Gatti, Carlo. <u>The Ferry to Capri</u>. Trans. Mario Della Bella. New York: Schocken, 1980.

> Della Bella, Mario, trans. <u>The Ferry to Capri</u>. By Carlo Gatti. New York: Schocken, 1980.

> Gatti, Carlo. <u>"The Amphitheater" and Other Stories</u>. Trans. Rosa Valentino. Ed. Leonard R. Jarvis. Washington: Steinman, 1981.

Two or more books by the same "author(s)"

Sometimes two or more entries in your Works Cited listing have *exactly* the same names at the beginning for the person(s) or the group responsible for the piece you're documenting. This could be because of repetition of a single author, a particular set of multiple authors, a group, a government or international body, editor(s), or translator(s)—whatever the name(s) that begin the entry. In such a case, give the name(s) only for the first entry; in following entries type *three hyphens* and a period in place of the name(s). *The three hyphens signify the same name(s),* so, for instance, if a person is named first as an author and next as a translator, you should use the three hyphens for the name in the second entry, following the hyphens with a comma and "trans." (Notice that in the samples below, their order is determined by the alphabetical order of their titles, since the "author" block is the same for each.)

> Cross, Amanda. <u>The Bulls of Minos</u>. Washington: Spinnaker, 1981.

> ---. <u>Complete Poems</u>. Washington: Spinnaker, 1984.

> ---, trans. <u>"Rio" and Other Poems</u>. By Vicente Martinez. New York: Shirlington, 1985.

However, if an entry with a single name is followed by an entry in which the first of multiple authors is that same name, do not use the three hyphens in the second entry. Three hyphens can signify more than one name, but the name block in each case must be *exactly* the same; thus, the three hyphens in the third sample on the following page stand for "Della Bella, Mario, and Rosa Valentino."

Della Bella, Mario, trans. <u>The Ferry to Capri</u>. By Carlo Gatti. New York: Schocken, 1980.

Della Bella, Mario, and Rosa Valentino, trans. <u>The Coast Road</u>. By Luigi Mautone. Washington: Steinman, 1983.

---, trans. <u>Tarantella</u>. By Carlo Gatti. New York: Schocken, 1985.

Finally, the three hyphens also should be used when groups, governments, or international bodies serve as "authors." And since government entries begin with the government and the name of the body or agency sponsoring the work, you may need more than one set of hyphens. The samples below illustrate the "author" blocks for several government publications in a row:

Indiana. Dept. of Revenue.

---. Dept. of Transportation.

United States. Cong. House.

---. ---. Senate.

---. Dept. of Energy.

Extratextual material

In citations for such extratextual material as an Introduction or Afterword, give the name of the author of that division of the book, followed by the name of the extratextual piece; the author of the work itself follows the title. If the author of the extratextual material is the same as the author of the book, give only the last name after the book title, as in the second example. Notice that both samples include inclusive page numbers for the named extratextual section of the book.

Carter, Sharron. Introduction. <u>The Chronicle of Eleanor</u>. By Sean Bordy. Baltimore: Court, 1984. i-xvi.

Wirth, Laura J. Afterword. <u>The Nautilus Cup</u>. By Wirth. Washington: Slay, 1983. 283-92.

Part of a collection

For parts of anthologies, collections of articles, and casebooks, the title of the piece precedes the title of the work. Normally the title of the piece will appear in quotation marks; however, if it was published originally as a book, underline it instead. Notice that as for an extratextual section of a book, above, the inclusive pages for the piece of the collection end the citation.

> Ostrowski, William N. "Tracing the Beaker Culture." <u>European Historical Studies</u>. Ed. Lawrence Winters. Ann Arbor: U of Michigan P, 1985. 372-407.

Cross-references

If you're documenting multiple pieces from the same collection, you have a choice. You can treat each piece as a part of a collection, giving full data for the collection itself each time. Or you can give one entry for the collection and then simplify the citations for the pieces by referring to the entry for the collection. Keep in mind, however, that one way or the other each specific piece of the collection that you refer to in the text of your paper requires its own entry in the Works Cited section of your research paper. Thus, with cross-references you save repeating some information in each of the citations for a piece of the collection, but you then must add an entry for the collection itself.

> Ostrowski, William N. "Tracing the Beaker Culture." Winters 372-407.

> Parker, Sheila T. "Sutton Hoo and Other Anglo-Saxon Ship Burials." Winters 164-92.

> Winters, Lawrence, ed. <u>European Historical Studies</u>. Ann Arbor: U of Michigan P, 1985.

Republished books

If you use a republished book (a new publication of an out-of-print book or a paperback version of a book originally published in hardcover), show the original publication date before the new publication information.

> Picot, Andrea. <u>Italian Chamber Music</u>. 1963. Washington: Spinnaker, 1984.

Edition other than first

Readers will assume the book is a first edition unless you indicate otherwise, such as second edition (2nd ed.), alternate edition (Alt. ed.), revised edition (Rev. ed.), and so on.

> Hruska, Allen S., Jr. <u>All About Personal Computers</u>. 3rd ed. Baltimore: Court, 1985.

Series

If a book is part of a series, give the series name and the number of the work in the series.

> Sloane, Mark. The Barrows of Stonehenge. Studies in Anthropology, No. 7. Albuquerque: La Madera, 1983.

Multivolume work

Despite the various possibilities below for citations of works with two or more volumes, all include the total number of volumes as amplifying information.

For a specific page reference to a multivolume work, the parenthetical reference in the text of your paper usually will include the volume number with the page reference (e.g., 2:76–77). However, if in your paper you never need to document from more than one volume of the set, you can end the Works Cited entry with the volume number (as below) and give only page references in the text itself (e.g., 76–77 instead of 2:76–77).

> Garrett, Thomas. Pottery and Decorations of the Mimbres. 2 vols. Arlington: Burning Tree, 1985. Vol. 2.

If the single volume you cite for your paper has its own title, include the specific volume reference between the individual and multivolume set titles, as below. Again, references in the text of your paper need not include the volume number.

> Moore, Tanya. European Imitations of Oriental Porcelains. Vol. 2 of The Development of Porcelains in Europe. 4 vols. New York: Westhaven Art, 1983.

If your paper requires references to two or more volumes, then use the more general multivolume citation in Works Cited (as below) and include the volume number with each parenthetical reference in the text of your paper.

> Garrett, Thomas. Pottery and Decorations of the Mimbres. 2 vols. Arlington: Burning Tree, 1985.

If the volumes of the multivolume work were published over a period of years, then the publication date block should show the first and last years of the set, as here:

> Silberstein, Gary M. The Roman Army in Britain. 4 vols. London: Chesterton, 1978-85.

If the multivolume set has not been completed, include "to date" with the number of volumes and follow the publication date of the first volume with a hyphen and a space:

> Keller, Jane Lee. <u>Renaissance Music</u>. 4 vols. to date. Washington: Luke, 1980- .

When you cite a piece in a multivolume collection of pieces, show the volume number with the inclusive page numbers for the specific part of the work:

> McGregor, David. "Arthur Wellesley in the Campaign Against Tippoo Sultan." <u>The Military Career of the Duke of Wellington</u>. Ed. Walter Miller. 3 vols. London: Westminster, 1982. 2:161-89.

Published conference proceedings

If the book title doesn't include information about the conference, provide amplifying information after the title.

> <u>Prospects for Computer Security</u>. Proc. of a Conference of the American Association of Computer Programmers. 18-22 Feb. 1985. Chicago: U of Chicago, 1985.

Pamphlet

Treat pamphlets as books.

> Rucker, Paul. <u>Antietam: Battle Plan and Monuments</u>. Boston: Liberty, 1984.

Missing publishing or pagination data

Use the following abbreviations for missing publication or pagination information: no place of publication: n.p.; no publisher: n.p.; no date: n.d.; no pagination: n.pag. The abbreviations for "no place" and "no publisher" are the same, but their positions left or right of the colon will allow readers to tell the difference. When a book has no pagination indicated, your Works Cited entry needs to contain "N.pag." so that readers will understand why parenthetical references in the text of your paper do not show page numbers.

> <u>Public Domain Computer Software</u>. N.p.: n.p., 1985. N.pag.

ENTRIES FOR ARTICLES IN PERIODICALS

Periodicals are publications that are issued periodically on some sort of schedule–quarterly, bimonthly, monthly, weekly, daily, and so forth. Authorities group periodicals into three classes: journals, magazines, and newspapers. Newspapers are easy to recognize, but you may have difficulty distinguishing between journals and magazines.

Many journals don't have the word *journal* in their titles, and not all periodicals with *journal* in their titles are considered journals for documentation. Nevertheless, some differentiation is necessary because the data required after the "publishing information" differs for the various types of periodicals. Fortunately, we don't need a scholarly distinction; instead we can make fairly simple divisions based on how the periodicals paginate their issues and on how frequently they publish issues. Therefore, the formats for the sample entries for periodicals can be distinguished on the following bases:

- *A periodical paged continuously throughout a volume is treated as a "journal, with continuous pagination."* If, for example, the first issue of a particular volume ends with page 156 and the next issue begins with page 157, the periodical uses continuous pagination throughout a volume.

- *When each issue of the periodical is paginated independently, it is treated as a "journal" if it is published less frequently than once every two months.* If each issue of a periodical begins with page 1, issues are paginated independently.

- *All other periodicals are distinguished by frequency of publication.*

GENERAL FORM: ARTICLES IN PERIODICALS

Group 1: Person(s) or group responsible for the piece of material you are documenting

- *Author(s).* If an article is signed, the name(s)—sometimes only initials—will appear either at the beginning or at the end of the article. Treat multiple authors as you would for book entries.

Group 2: The title(s)

- *Title of article.* See pages 140–142 for guidance on capitalization, quotation marks, and underlining in titles.

Group 3: Amplifying information, to help identify or describe the work precisely

- *Type of article.* You'll need this only for editorials, letters to the editor, and reviews.

Group 4: Publishing information, or similar information that will help someone find the work

- *Name of periodical.* The name of the periodical itself is all the publishing information that is necessary. Drop any introductory article from the title, but add the institution or, particularly for newspapers, the city in square brackets after the title if readers aren't likely to recognize the title itself.

Group 5: Identification of the portion you are citing

- *Series number.* If a journal has been published in more than one series (e.g., original and new), indicate the applicable series. Otherwise readers may have difficulty determining where to find the article you used.
- *Newspaper edition.* If a newspaper has both morning and evening or special editions, you may need to show which you used; check the masthead of the newspaper when you read it. The same article often will appear in more than one edition, but not necessarily in the same place in each.
- *Volume and/or issue number(s).* For *journals,* you'll include the volume and/or issue number for the issue you used.
- *Date.* All entries will include at least the year, but whether year only, month and year, or complete date depends on the type of periodical.
- *Page number(s).* See pages 142–143 for guidance on showing inclusive page numbers.

SAMPLE ENTRIES: ARTICLES IN PERIODICALS

As with the samples for books, the following entries were designed to illustrate particular portions of documentation entries. You may want to adapt the formats to fit your needs, but be sure to include all pertinent information listed in the preceding discussion of general form. NOTE: The three-hyphen form for repeated "author" (see "Two or More Books by the Same 'Author(s)'" on pages 127–128) applies to entries for articles in periodicals as well, but is not repeated below.

Journal with continuous pagination

This type of entry includes the volume number followed by the year in parentheses, a colon, and then inclusive page numbers for the article.

Brennan, James. "The Solitude of Gabriel Garcia Marquez." <u>Studies in Latin American Fiction</u> 8 (1984): 316-36.

Journal with issues paged independently

To the volume number, add a period and the issue number.

Harris, Dianne. "Emblematic Figures in William Blake's Portrayals of the Works of John Milton." <u>European Painting</u> 11.2 (1985): 38-61.

Journal with issue numbers only

If a journal does not use volume numbers, use the issue number as if it were a volume number.

Mills, Bruce. "The 'Great Bed of Ware' in the Writings of Shakespeare and His Comtemporaries." <u>Shakespeare Journal</u> 3 (1984): 15-22.

Journal with series

If a journal has been published in more than one series, show the series before the volume number. Use "ns" and "os" for "new series" and "original series," or a numerical designator such as "3rd ser."

Llosa, Julio. "The Spread of Maiolica in Europe." <u>Ceramic Arts</u> ns 5 (1985): 372-86.

Monthly or bimonthly periodical

Instead of volume and/or issue, use month(s) and year.

Novinski, Eric. "Programming Music on Your PC." <u>Computers at Home</u> Feb. 1985: 115-32.

Weekly or biweekly periodicals

Whether magazine or newspaper, for a periodical published once a week or once every two weeks, give the complete date rather than volume and issue numbers.

Phipps, Beverly. "Ludlow Man: Garroted and Dumped in a Peat Bog Almost 3000 Years Ago." <u>Musuem News</u> 14 Dec. 1984: 12-16.

Daily newspaper

Show the newspaper's name as it appears at the top of the first page, omitting any beginning article (e.g., *The Washington Post* becomes *Washington Post*) except for *The New York Times,* which retains the article. If the newspaper's title doesn't name the city, give the city and state in square brackets after the title, as in the first sample below. The first sample also illustrates how to indicate the edition for a newspaper that prints more than one edition a day (again, check the masthead on the first page to see if an edition is given).

For inclusive page numbers, check the pagination system of the newspaper carefully. If the newspaper doesn't have sections or if it numbers continuously through the edition, you'll need only page numbers after the date (e.g., 12 Dec. 1985: 23). If the newspaper includes the section number with the page numbers, the appropriate section-number combinations can follow the date (e.g., 12 Dec. 1984: A11–A12). But if the section designator is not combined with the page number, then show the section designator between the date and the page number(s) (e.g., 12 Dec. 1984, sec. 2: 17).

Coleman, Joanne. "Violence Changes Community." <u>Tribune</u> [Dover, MI] 5 Sep. 1984, sunrise ed.: 17-18.

Faruk, Abdul. "War of Attrition Between Iran and Iraq." <u>Washington Post</u> 23 Nov. 1985: B16.

Author unknown

Whatever the type of periodical, if no author is given, begin with the article's title. The format for the rest of the entry, of course, depends on the type of periodical in which the article appears; the sample below is for a monthly magazine.

"New Discoveries at Herculaneum." <u>Ancient History</u> Sep. 1984: 53-67.

Editorial

Begin with the author if named, otherwise with the editorial's title, and follow the title with "Editorial" (without quotation marks). The rest of the entry depends on the source; our sample uses a daily newspaper.

"Will Iran Consider Peace?" Editorial. <u>Washington Post</u> 17
    Sep. 1985: A15

Letter to the editor

Letters to editors can appear in any type of periodical, so the portion
after the title depends on the type of publication in which the letter appears. We show a journal (with continuous pagination).

Burrows, Edward. Letter. <u>Journal of Antiquity</u> 10 (1985):
    276.

Review

Reviews may be signed or unsigned and titled or untitled, and they
may appear in any type of periodical. For a signed review, use the
name(s) of the reviewer(s), the review title (if there is one), and then
"Rev. of . . . ." For an unsigned review, give the title (if there is one); if
not, begin with "Rev. of . . . ." The first entry below shows a signed and
titled review in a monthly magazine; the second sample is for an unsigned, untitled review in a daily newspaper.

Gonzalez, Maria. "The Art of Cave Art." Rev. of <u>Paleolithic
    Mural Art in Europe</u>, by Elizabeth Korden. Ancient His-
    tory Nov. 1985: 83-85.

Rev. of <u>The Nautilus Cup</u>, by Laura J. Wirth. <u>Washington Post</u>
    8 Dec. 1984: D5

ENTRIES FOR OTHER SOURCES

GENERAL FORM: OTHER SOURCES

This mixed group of reference types lacks a standard form. Still, the general idea for all documentation entries applies: (1) person(s) or group
responsible for the piece of material you're documenting; (2) the title(s);
(3) amplifying information, to help identify or describe the work precisely; (4) publishing information, or similar information that will help
someone find the work; and (5) identification of the portion you are citing. These miscellaneous documentation entries follow those general
guidelines.

SAMPLE ENTRIES: OTHER SOURCES

If there isn't a sample that fits your needs exactly, adapt entries or create
a format, but keep the general guidelines in mind.

Speech

Use the speech title, if known; when it isn't, use in its place a designator such as Address, Keynote speech, or Lecture. Titles, as in the first sample, go in quotation marks, of course, but the descriptive designators are used without quotation marks, as in the second sample.

> Eilberg, Rebecca. "Leadership and Enjoyment: They Don't Have to Conflict." Conference of the National Association of American Girl Scout Leaders in Europe. Verona, Italy, 8 Sep. 1985.

> Kendall, Melissa. Keynote speech. Conference of the National Association of American Girl Scout Leaders in Europe. Verona, Italy, 8 Sep. 1985.

Class handout or lecture

Show class, place, and date; as appropriate and available, give speaker and title.

> "Elements of Perspective." Art 102 handout. Smithfield College, 1985.

> Dyer, Richard. Music 211 lecture. Eastern U, 7 Mar. 1984.

Reference work

Entries for items in standard reference works require less information than do entries for books. For a signed encyclopedia article, give author, article title, encyclopedia title, and edition. For an unsigned article, begin with the article title. If citations are for encyclopedias or dictionaries that alphabetize articles, volume and page references are unnecessary. Of course, if the encyclopedia has separate major divisions, each of which has articles in alphabetical order, include the division title with the encyclopedia title (e.g., *Encyclopaedia Britannica: Macropaedia*). For other standard reference works, such as one of the *Who's Who* series, give only the edition, if applicable, and publication year after the title (e.g., 12th ed. 1982–83.). However, treat an article in a less common reference work as a piece in a book collection (see "Part of a Collection," pages 128–129), and give full publication information.

> "Stonehenge." <u>Encyclopedia Americana</u>. 1984 ed.

Computer software

For commercially produced computer software, begin with the writer of the program, if available; if not, begin with the title. Label with the term "Computer software," and give as a minimum the distributor and publication year. Optional information may be added at the end of the entry. This information may include the computer for which the program is designed, the operating system, and whether the program is on cartridge, cassette, or disk.

> Filefolder Data Base Management. Computer software. Scienobyte, 1985. Macintosh disk.

Material from a computer or information service

Material from a computer service (such as DIALOG, Mead, or BRS) or an information service (such as ERIC or NTIS) is like other printed material, but after the publishing information you need to add a reference to the service, giving its name and the accession or order number for the material you're citing. Thus, most of the sample entry below corresponds to a document that is part of a series, while the end of the entry refers to the information service.

> Stephens, Harold. An Argument for Sectioning by Ability. Classroom Education Techniques, No. 3. Syracuse: Syracuse UP, 1975. ERIC ED 041 216.

Unpublished thesis or dissertation

When a thesis or dissertation has been published, treat it as a book. However, if you use an unpublished form, show the type of work, the institution for which it was prepared, and the year it was accepted. Note that the title appears in quotation marks because the work is unpublished.

> Taylor, Kristen. "The Arthur Legend in Medieval Chronicles." Diss. U of Nebraska, 1985.

Unpublished letter

Treat a published letter as a part of a book collection or as a letter in a periodical. The first entry below shows the format for a letter you yourself have received. The second illustrates an unpublished letter in an archive.

> Anderson, Virginia. Letter to the author. 16 Apr. 1984.

> Dean, George B. Letter to Robert James Webb. 17 Mar. 1866. Robert James Webb Collection. Hurley Museum Library. Huntington, SC.

Interview

To document an interview you have conducted, begin with the name of the person interviewed, show the type of interview (personal or telephone), and give the date it was held.

> Cotrel, Andre. Personal interview. 5 Dec. 1984.

Film, filmstrip, slide program, videocassette

For a film, usually you'll begin with the title, followed by the director, distributor, and year released. Other information (stars, writers, and so on) is optional but should be included if it bears on how you discuss the film in your paper; put this information as amplification after the director. However, if your paper deals with the work of a particular individual connected with the film, begin with that person.

For a filmstrip, slide program, or videocassette, show the type of medium after the title, and then follow the format for a film citation.

> Winston Before Five. Dir. Hae Chiong Lee. Panorama, 1985.

> The Outer Banks. Videocassette. Dir. Ruth Owens. Video Concepts, 1985.

Radio or television program

As a minimum, give the program title, the network that aired it, the local station and city for the broadcast that you viewed or heard, and the broadcast date. An episode title, if available, can be shown in quotation marks preceding the program title (as in our sample), and a series title, with no special markings, can be shown after the program title. Other information may be added for amplification, and if your paper deals with the work of a particular person connected with the broadcast, begin the entry with that individual's name.

> "Teenage Suicide." Weekend Newsline. ABC. WCAM, Cincinnati. 12 Oct. 1985.

Record or tape

Begin the entry with the person you want to emphasize (speaker, author, composer, producer, and so on); then give the title and follow it with "Audiotape" if your source is a tape rather than a record. Show the artists (along with any appropriate amplification), the manufacturer, identification number, and release year.

> Cross, Amanda. The Bulls of Minos. Audiotape. Read by Julia Kowalski. Recorded Books, 80068, 1983.

Legal citations

Complex legal citations are beyond the scope of this volume. Consult the Harvard Law Review Association's *A Uniform System of Citation* for help. The sample entries below are for federal statutory material; both use section references rather than page references. Use similar entries for state constitutions and statutes.

> 5 US Code. Sec. 522a. 1974.

> US Const. Art. 3, sec. 1.

Citations for law cases show the names of first plantiff and first defendant, the volume of the report being cited, the name of the report, the page of the report, the name of the court where the case was decided, and the year decided.

> Jefferson v. Sommers. 155 AS 613. Ind. Ct. App. 1978.

SPECIAL RULES FOR TITLES

CAPITALIZATION

Use capital letters for the *first letters* of the following types of words in titles:

- *Each important word in the title (see below for "unimportant" words).*
- *The first word in a title (e.g., "A House on Tatum Hill").*
- *The first word after a colon that joins a title and a subtitle (e.g., "Faulkner's 'Delta Autumn': The Fall of Idealism").*
- *Parts of compound words that would be capitalized if they appeared by themselves (e.g., "School Declares All-Out War on Misspelling").*

Don't use capital letters for the following unimportant words:

- *The articles* a, an *and* the.
- *Short prepositions such as* at, by, for, in, of, on, to, up.
- *The conjunctions* and, as, but, if, nor, or, for, so, yet.
- *The second element of a compound numeral (e.g., "Twenty-five Years of Tyranny").*

NEITHER QUOTATION MARKS NOR UNDERLINING

Don't use either quotation marks or underlining (or italics) for the following:

- *The Bible, the books of the Bible, and other sacred works such as the Talmud or the Koran.*

- *Legal references (such as acts, laws, and court cases).*
- *Extratextual material in a book (such as the Introduction or Foreword).*

UNDERLINING

Printers usually use italics, but in typing you use underlining for certain types of titles (unless, of course, you're using computerized word processing that gives you a capability for italic type; then you, too, can use italics). Underline the title of works published separately—such as novels and poems that are entire books or pamphlets—and the titles of periodicals (magazines, journals, and newspapers). Also underline the titles of movies and radio or television programs.

QUOTATION MARKS

Use quotation marks to enclose titles of works such as short stories, most poems, and essays that are published as parts of other works. Also, include titles of speeches and class lectures in quotation marks.

If, however, a work that has been published separately appears as part of a larger work—such as a play or novel as part of an anthology— underline (or italicize) the title. For example, underline Voltaire's *Candide* even when it is part of an anthology entitled *Great Works of World Literature*.

MIXED QUOTATION MARKS AND UNDERLINING

You have to adapt the rules somewhat when one title appears within another. The following samples illustrate the markings for the four possible combinations of titles with quotation marks and titles with underlining (or italics):

"Faulkner's 'Delta Autumn': The Fall of Idealism"

This is a short story title within an essay title: Each title without the other would have double quotation marks, but here the title within a title has single quotation marks.

Faulkner's "Delta Autumn" and the Myth of the Wilderness

This is a short story title within a book title: Each title has its normal markings.

"Laertes as Foil in Hamlet"

This is a play title within an essay title: Each title has its normal markings.

Shakespeare's "Hamlet": Action Versus Contemplation

This is a play within a book title: The title within a title, which by itself would be underlined, here has double quotation marks.

SPECIAL RULES FOR PUBLISHERS' NAMES

SHORTENING

Follow these rules in shortening publishers' names for your Works Cited entries:

- *Omit the articles* a, an, the.
- *Omit business designators such as* Co., Inc., *or* Ltd.
- *Omit labels such as* Books, Press, *or* Publishers. NOTE: University presses are exceptions. Since both universities and their presses may publish independently, use *P* for *Press* when the publisher is a university press (thus, *Indiana U* is distinct from *Indiana UP*).
- *If the publisher's name includes the name of one person, use only the last name* (Alfred A. Knopf, Inc. *becomes* Knopf).
- *If the name includes several people, use only the first of the names* (Holt, Rinehart and Winston *becomes* Holt).
- *Use the following standard abbreviations:* UP *for University Press;* GPO *for Government Printing Office;* HMSO *for Her (His) Majesty's Stationery Office;* MLA *for the Modern Language Association of America;* NAL *for The New American Library;* NCTE *for the National Council of Teachers of English; and* NEA *for The National Education Association.*

IMPRINTS

When the title page or copyright page of a book shows a publisher's special imprint, combine the imprint with a shortened version of the publisher's name: for example, a *Sentry Edition* published by *Houghton Mifflin Company* becomes *Sentry-Houghton;* a *Mentor Book* published by *The New American Library, Inc.,* becomes *Mentor-NAL.*

SPECIAL RULES FOR INCLUSIVE PAGE NUMBERS

When you give inclusive page references, often you can shorten the second number. Up to 100, include all digits (e.g., 3–4, 54–55). Thereafter, reduce the second number of a set to two digits (e.g., 253–54, 304–05,

2614–15) *unless* the hundred or thousand changes (e.g., 499–501, 2998–3002).

EXERCISE

Prepare a Works Cited page to include entries for the works below:

1. An article entitled "Who's Afraid of Virginia's Computer?" This article, by Melissa N. Kendall, appeared on pages 62 to 74 of issue 10, October 1985, of *Business World.* This magazine is published monthly.

2. A book by Jessica Merrill entitled *Computer Security* and subtitled *A Guide for Industry.* This book was published in 1985 by the University of Chicago.

3. Another book by Jessica Merrill, this one called *Artificial Intelligence and the Computer.* The book was published by Shirlington Press, of New York City, in 1984.

4. An article on pages 33 to 42 of the 19 July 1985 issue of *American Industry News,* a weekly magazine. No author was given for the article, which was entitled "New Entry Code Judged Too Complex for Employees, Too Simple for Hackers."

5. *Applications for Personal Computers,* a two-volume work by Barbara Gibson. Both volumes were published in 1984 by Steinman Brothers, Inc., of Washington, DC.

6. A journal article entitled "Breaking the Code: Hackers and Computer Security." This article, by Gerald P. Olson, appeared on pages 412 through 436 of volume 5, the Spring 1984 issue, of *Computers in Business,* a journal that paginates continuously throughout a volume.

7. An editorial entitled "Do We Need Artificial Intelligence?" This unsigned editorial appeared on page A12 of the *Denver Post* on 9 November 1985.

8. A book by the Association of American Businesses entitled *Guidelines on Security for Computers in Business,* published in 1983 in Washington, DC, by the Association of American Businesses.

9. An article entitled "Business Graphics on the Small Computer," which appeared on pages 192 through 209 of a collection of essays entitled *The Personal Computer in Business and Industry.* The article was written by Michael Anderson. Helen S. Roy edited the collection of essays, which was published in 1983 by Holt, Rinehart and Winston of New York.

11

Documentation with Notes

If you're using parenthetical documentation for your research paper, you probably won't need to read this chapter. If, however, you find you must use notes to support the text of your research paper—in addition to using parenthetical documentation to provide place references to your sources—you can find instructions in this chapter on how to place note numbers in the text of your paper and how to present footnotes at the bottom of the page on which they occur.

On the other hand, if your instructor wants you to document your paper with notes rather than with parenthetical references, then this chapter is especially for you. Here you'll learn about the format conventions associated with *documentation with notes*, a traditional style of documentation reference that some instructors prefer to the parenthetical reference system.

Documentation with notes involves interaction of the following three portions of your research paper:

- *Note numbers in the text of your paper.* These mark the location in your text where the note citation applies and provide a numerical reference to the body of the note citation.

- *Footnotes or endnotes.* Footnotes are note citations at the bottoms of the pages where documentation references occur; endnotes collect all note citations in a page or pages after the body of your paper. In both cases they detail specific portion references of the sources supporting your text.

- *Works Cited or Bibliography.* Whatever the name, this is an alphabetized listing of all the sources supporting your research paper. This list provides a general reference to your sources but, of course, doesn't identify the specific portions you used for the quotations, paraphrases, and summaries in the body of your paper.

DOCUMENTATION AND SUPPORT NOTES

Most notes are for *documentation*—to tell readers the precise place in a source for the material you are summarizing, paraphrasing, or quoting. However, other notes also can *support* your paper with discussion of sources that agree or disagree with the point you're making. Here's a sample support note:

> [1]Sloane agrees with Palin that most purchasers of personal computers have not determined how they will use the computer before they buy it; see John J. Sloane, "A Guide for Beginners in Choosing and Buying a Personal Computer," Computers at Home Jan. 1985: 73. See also T. Randolph Webb, Your Computer and You (New York: Schocken, 1984) 15; Evelyn Martin, Home Computers (Washington: Slay, 1984) 227-28; and Jackson M. Roy, Buying a Personal Computer (New York: Shirlington, 1985) 7.

Since this type of discussion would create a disruptive digression in the text itself, it should be placed in a support note or left out of the paper altogether (and leaving out such digressions often is the better choice). If you need support notes, include them with the more prevalent documentation notes; no special numbering or format is necessary.

PLACING NOTE NUMBERS IN THE TEXT

Following are rules for placing the note numbers (commonly referred to as "footnote numbers") in the body of your paper:

- *Number notes consecutively throughout the paper.* Do not reuse a number; for example, the fifth note will be numbered 5 even if its content matches exactly that of note number 2.

- *Use Arabic numerals (1, 2, 3, etc.) as reference marks in the body of the paper.*

- *Type each number so it will appear to be raised roughly one-half space above the line—like this [3]—as a* superscript *figure.* Do not space before the number—like this [3]—and do not embellish the number with slashes, parentheses, periods, hand-drawn circles, or any other marks. However, do put the number after all punctuation marks except dashes. (NOTE: If you're using computerized word processing to prepare your research paper, see how your software treats superscript characters. Some programs do not actually raise the superscript characters one-half space above the normal line of type. They should, however, present superscript characters so they appear raised and distinctly different from normal type. You may need to print a sample and get your instructor to approve its appearance.)

- *Always put the number* after *the material to which it refers.* Put the number as close as reasonably possible to the end of the material you're documenting, but always at the end of a clause or phrase so it doesn't seem to interrupt. (The concept for placing note numbers in the text is the same as that for placing parenthetical references in the text in the parenthetical documentation system; you may find it useful to read the disussion called "Placement in Text" beginning on page 116 of Chapter 9.)

FOOTNOTES AND ENDNOTES

You have a choice of whether to type the note citations themselves at the bottoms of the appropriate pages as footnotes or to gather them into one listing (called Notes) as endnotes after all the text pages. If you choose *footnotes,* here's how to format the bottom of a page on which notes occur (in this case, notes 1 and 2):

Last line of text on the page.

――――――――――――

[1]Thomas Garrett, <u>Pottery and Decorations of the Mimbres,</u> 2 vols. (Arlington: Burning Tree, 1985) 2:53.

where: who   when vol page

[2]Gayle Adams and Terri Beals, <u>Aztec Funereal Art</u> (Austin: U of Texas P, 1983) 119.

1 in.

- *Stay within the normal margins for a page of text.*
- *After the last line of text, single-space and then type a line twenty spaces long, beginning at the left margin of the page.* This line sets the note citations off visually from the text on the page.

- *After typing the dividing line, double-space to find the line on which to begin the first note.*
- *Indent the first line of each note five spaces, just as you do the first line of a paragraph.* All subsequent lines of each note, however, return to the left margin.
- *Raise the note number half a line.*
- *Single-space within each note, but double-space between notes.*

Easier to type, however, is a Notes section, a page or more at the end of your paper (after the text but before the Works Cited or Bibliography pages), putting all the notes from the paper in one place. Since the Notes section puts your notes at the end of the paper, technically they are then *endnotes*. However, the contents of both footnotes and endnotes are the same; only the layout on the page changes.

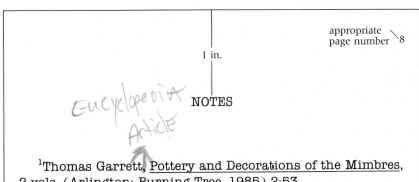

appropriate
page number ＼8

1 in.

ᴇɴᴄʏᴄʟᴏᴘᴇᴅɪᴀ
ᴀʀᴛɪᴄʟᴇ   NOTES

¹Thomas Garrett, <u>Pottery and Decorations of the Mimbres</u>, 2 vols. (Arlington: Burning Tree, 1985) 2:53.

²Gayle Adams and Terri Beals, <u>Aztec Funereal Art</u> (Austin: U of Texas P, 1983) 119.

¹⁷Garrett 1:233.

1 in.

- *Use the same margins as for the rest of the pages of your research paper.*
- *Triple-space from the centered title ''Notes'' to find the line on which to begin the first note.*

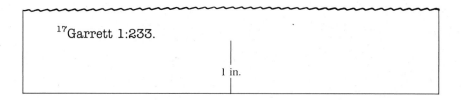

3 "ᴀʀᴛɪᴄʟᴇ," ᴄʏᴄʟᴇ
ɴᴏᴠᴇᴍʙᴇʀ 1983, ᴘᴘ. 84-88

- *Indent the first line of each note five spaces, but return all subsequent lines of each note to the left margin.*
- *Raise each note number half a line.*
- *Single-space each note, but double-space between notes.*

WORKS CITED OR BIBLIOGRAPHY

Traditional use of documentation with notes also demands inclusion in your paper of a complete *general source listing* of the sources used to support the paper. This lising can be called "Works Cited," as it usually is with parenthetical documentation, or your instructor may prefer "Bibliography" or "Selected Bibliography." *Contents of individual bibliographic entries are the same as for entries in Works Cited described in Chapter 10.* The general source listing—whatever you name it—follows the Notes section of your research paper. Format the Works Cited or Bibliography page(s) as shown in Chapter 10, pages 120–121.

DOCUMENTATION NOTE FORMAT

Most differences between a note entry and the Works Cited entry to which it corresponds are in format. Study the matched entries below and see whether you can spot the differences.

Works Cited:

Garrett, Thomas. <u>Pottery and Decorations of the Mimbres</u>. 2
    vols. Arlington: Burning Tree, 1985.

Note:

[1]Thomas Garrett, <u>Pottery and Decorations of the Mimbres</u>,
2 vols. (Arlington: Burning Tree, 1985) 2:53.

- *The note has a number; the Works Cited entry doesn't.* Notes are numbered in order of appearance in the paper, while the Works Cited entries are arranged alphabetically.
- *The first line of the note is indented five spaces from the left margin and all other lines go to that margin.* For the Works Cited entry, only the first line goes to the left margin, and all subsequent lines are indented five spaces.

- *In a note the "author's" name (occasionally the editor, translator, etc.) is in normal order (first-middle-last).* In the Works Cited entry the "author's" last name comes first.

- *The note is like a sentence, so other than periods in abbreviations, the only period is at the end of the note.* In a Works Cited entry, each group of information ends with a period.

- *Publishing information in a note is in parentheses.* This is not the case for the Works Cited entry.

- *The note ends with a specific reference to a page or pages.* A Works Cited entry either gives no page numbers (as in the book entry used here) or gives the inclusive pages for an entire article (for a piece in a collection or for an article in a periodical). Of course, for non-print sources, such as a film or lecture, neither the note nor the Works Cited entry could show pagination.

SAMPLE NOTE ENTRIES

As you can see above, the basic content of a note entry corresponds to the basic content of a Works Cited entry. Format changes, of course, but the substantive difference is in specific page reference for the note versus general page reference (none or inclusive pages) for the Works Cited entry. Thus, the logic behind what you need to include in your notes is the same as that detailed for Works Cited entries in Chapter 10—both the general forms and specific samples. Following, then, are sample note entries that correspond to the sample Works Cited entries in Chapter 10. We've retained the order from Chapter 10 to make cross-references easier for you.

SAMPLE NOTES FOR FIRST FULL REFERENCES TO BOOKS

One author

[1]Warren Stein, <u>Art of the Ancient Peoples of Latin America</u> (Albuquerque: La Madera, 1984) 82.

Two or three authors

[2]Gayle Adams and Terri Beals, <u>Aztec Funereal Art</u> (Austin: U of Texas P, 1983) 119.

[3]Bruce Mills, Frank J. Jensen, and Larry S. Wilson, Jr., Gemstones and Medieval Medicinal Magic (New York: Schocken, 1985) 137.

More than three authors

[4]Melissa Kendall, et al., The Amber Wars and the Development of Europe (New York: Shirlington, 1984) 23-24.

Group as author

[5]National Commission on Aging, Report of the National Commission on Aging (Washington: GPO, 1982) 314.

Government and international body publications

[6]United States, Dept. of State, Islamic Organizations and Stability in the Middle East, by Shirley Fitzsimmons (Washington: GPO, 1985) 73-74.

[7]Shirley Fitzsimmons, Islamic Organizations and Stability in the Middle East, U.S. Dept. of State (Washington: GPO, 1985) 73-74.

[8]Cong. Rec., 8 May 1979: 2756-57.

[9]United States, Cong., House, Permanent Select Committee on Intelligence, Technological Transfer Losses in the 1970s, 102nd Cong., 2nd sess., H. Rept. 1122 (Washington: GPO, 1983) 115.

[10]United Nations, Committee for Economic Cooperation, Mineral Development in Southern Africa (Elmsford: Pergamon, 1984) 256.

Author not given

[11]A Treasury of Russian Humor (Washington: Luke, 1984) 51.

Editor

[12]Emily Smith, English Stoneware, ed. Brooke Harter (Huntington, SC: Hurley Museum, 1981) 64.

[13]Brooke Harter, ed., English Stoneware, by Emily Smith (Huntington, SC: Hurley Museum, 1981) 64.

Translator

[14]Carlo Gatti, <u>The Ferry to Capri</u>, trans. Mario Della Bella (New York: Schocken, 1980) 85-86.

[15]Mario Della Bella, trans., <u>The Ferry to Capri</u>, by Carlo Gatti (New York: Schocken, 1980) 85-86.

[16]Carlo Gatti, <u>"The Amphitheater" and Other Stories</u>, trans. Rosa Valentino, ed. Leonard R. Jarvis (Washington: Steinman, 1981) 204.

Two or more books by the same "author(s)"

The fact that there are multiple listings alphabetized under the same name(s) in the Works Cited or Bibliography has no bearing on first full note references to any of the entries. Nothing in first full references in Notes corresponds to the three-hyphen system used for repeated names in Works Cited.

Extratextual material

[17]Sharron Carter, introduction, <u>The Chronicle of Eleanor</u>, by Sean Bordy (Baltimore: Court, 1984) xii.

[18]Laura J. Wirth, afterword, <u>The Nautilus Cup</u>, by Wirth (Washington: Slay, 1983) 290.

Part of a collection

[19]William N. Ostrowski, "Tracing the Beaker Culture," <u>European Historical Studies</u>, ed. Lawrence Winters (Ann Arbor: U of Michigan P, 1985) 403-04.

Cross-references

Whether you list each piece of a collection separately in Works Cited or list only the collection itself there, *all* first full note references to articles in collections require the full information for the article, as in sample note 19 above.

Republished books

[20]Andrea Picot, <u>Italian Chamber Music</u> (1963; Washington: Spinnaker, 1984) 138.

Edition other than first

[21]Allen S. Hruska, Jr., <u>All About Personal Computers</u>, 3rd. ed. (Baltimore: Court, 1985) 86.

Series

[22]Mark Sloane, <u>The Barrows of Stonehenge</u>, Studies in Anthropology, No. 7 (Albuquerque: La Madera, 1983) 157.

Multivolume works

Most note references to a specific place in a volume of a multivolume work require both the volume number and the page(s); notice, however, that sample note 24 below does not give the volume with the pages since a specific volume of the set is described in the contents of the note.

[23]Thomas Garrett, <u>Pottery and Decorations of the Mimbres</u>, 2 vols. (Arlington: Burning Tree, 1985) 2:221.

[24]Tanya Moore, <u>European Imitations of Oriental Porcelains</u>, vol. 2 of <u>The Development of Porcelains in Europe</u>, 4 vols. (New York: Westhaven Art, 1983) 115-16.

[25]Gary M. Silberstein, <u>The Roman Army in Britain</u>, 4 vols. (London: Chesterton, 1978-85) 3:223.

[26]Jane Lee Keller, <u>Renaissance Music</u>, 4 vols. to date (Washington: Luke, 1980-), 1:177.

[27]David McGregor, "Arthur Wellesley in the Campaign Against Tippoo Sultan," <u>The Military Career of the Duke of Wellington</u>, ed. Walter Miller, 3 vols. (London: Westminister, 1982) 2:165.

Published conference proceedings

[28]<u>Prospects for Computer Security</u>, Proc. of a Conference of the American Association of Computer Programmers, 18-22 Feb. 1985 (Chicago: U of Chicago, 1985) 82.

Pamphlet

[29]Paul Rucker, <u>Antietam: Battle Plan and Monuments</u> (Boston: Liberty, 1984) 16.

Missing publishing or pagination data

Obviously, if pagination is lacking, as it is for the pamphlet here, the note has no page reference at the end.

[30]Public Domain Computer Software (N.p.: n.p., 1985).

SAMPLE NOTES FOR FIRST FULL REFERENCES TO ARTICLES IN PERIODICALS

Journal with continuous pagination

[31]James Brennan, "The Solitude of Gabriel Garcia Marquez," Studies in Latin American Fiction 8 (1984): 317.

Journal with issues paged independently

[32]Dianne Harris, "Emblematic Figures in William Blake's Portrayals of the Works of John Milton," European Painting 11.2 (1985): 38.

Journal with issue numbers only

[33]Bruce Mills, "The 'Great Bed of Ware' in the Writings of Shakespeare and His Contemporaries," Shakespeare Journal 3 (1984): 20.

Journal with series

[34]Julio Llosa, "The Spread of Maiolica in Europe," Ceramic Arts ns 5 (1985): 386.

Monthly or bimonthly periodical

[35]Eric Novinski, "Programming Music on Your PC," Computers at Home Feb. 1985: 117.

Weekly or biweekly periodical

[36]Beverly Phipps, "Ludlow Man: Garroted and Dumped in a Peat Bog Almost 3000 Years Ago," Museum News 14 Dec. 1984: 12.

Daily newspaper

[37]Joanne Coleman, "Violence Changes Community," Tribune (Dover, MI) 5 Sep. 1984, sunrise ed.: 17.

[38]Abdul Faruk, "War of Attrition Between Iran and Iraq," Washington Post 23 Nov. 1985: B16.

Author unknown

[39]"New Discoveries at Herculaneum," Ancient History Sep. 1984: 65.

Editorial

[40]"Will Iran Consider Peace?" editorial, Washington Post 17 Sep. 1985: A15.

Letter to the editor

[41]Edward Burrows, letter, Journal of Antiquity 10 (1985): 276.

Review

[42]Maria Gonzalez, "The Art of Cave Art," rev. of Paleolithic Mural Art in Europe, by Elizabeth Korden, Ancient History Nov. 1985: 83.

[43]Rev. of The Nautilus Cup, by Laura J. Wirth, Washington Post 8 Dec. 1984: D5.

SAMPLE NOTES FOR FIRST FULL REFERENCES TO OTHER SOURCES

Speech

[44]Rebecca Eilberg, "Leadership and Enjoyment: They Don't Have to Conflict," Conference of the National Association of American Girl Scout Leaders in Europe, Verona, Italy, 8 Sep. 1985.

[45]Melissa Kendall, keynote speech, Conference of the National Association of American Girl Scout Leaders in Europe, Verona, Italy, 8 Sep. 1985.

Class handout or lecture

[46]"Elements of Perspective," Art 102 handout, Smithfield College, 1985, 4.

[47]Richard Dyer, Music 211 lecture, Eastern U, 7 Mar. 1984.

Reference work

[48]"Stonehenge," Encyclopedia Americana, 1984 ed.

Computer software

[49]Filefolder Data Base Management, computer software, Scienobyte, 1985 (Macintosh disk).

Material from computer or information service

[50]Harold Stephens, An Argument for Sectioning by Ability, Classroom Education Techniques, No. 3 (Syracuse: Syracuse UP, 1975) 63 (ERIC ED 041 216).

Unpublished thesis or dissertation

[51]Kristen Taylor, "The Arthur Legend in Medieval Chronicles," diss., U of Nebraska, 1985, 212.

Unpublished letter

[52]Virginia Anderson, letter to the author, 16 Apr. 1984.

[53]George B. Dean, letter to Robert James Webb, 17 Mar. 1866, Robert James Webb Collection, Hurley Museum Library, Huntington, SC.

Interview

[55]Andre Cotrel, personal interview, 5 Dec. 1984.

Film, filmstrip, slide program, videocassette

[55]Winston Before Five, dir. Hae Chiong Lee, Panorama, 1985.

[56]The Outer Banks, videocassette, dir. Ruth Owens, Video Concepts, 1985.

Radio or television program

[57]"Teenage Suicide," Weekend Newsline, ABC, WCAM, Cincinnati, 12 Oct. 1985.

Record or tape

[58]Amanda Cross, The Bulls of Minos, audiotape, read by Julia Kowalski, Recorded Books, 80068, 1983.

Legal citation

[59]5 US Code, sec. 522a (1974).

[60]US Const., art. 3, sec. 1.

[61]Jefferson v. Sommers, 153 AS 613 (Ind. Ct. App. 1978).

Indirect reference

If you quote information from a source that quotes the original, your note for the quotation should include information about the original source.

[62]John Harris, Criticizing the Critics (New York: Schocken, 1962) 153, qtd. in John J. Armstrong, "What's Wrong with Detective Fiction?" American Fiction 11.2 (1981): 13.

SUBSEQUENT REFERENCES

After a first full reference to a source, subsequent note references to the same source should appear in shortened form. Use a shortened form of the opening of the full note reference and appropriate page reference, if any. Let's look again at our first sample note in its full form:

[1]Warren Stein, Art of the Ancient Peoples of Latin America (Albuquerque: La Madera, 1984) 82.

A second reference to this work would look like this:

[63]Stein, 93.

If there had already been references to more than one book by Warren Stein, we'd give a little more information to identify which book we were noting:

[64]Stein, Art of the Ancient Peoples of Latin America 93.

And if the first full note for a work began with the title instead of a name, we'd begin the subsequent reference with the title (or a shortened version of it). Here's a subsequent reference to the anonymous magazine article that appeared in sample note 39 above.

[65]"New Discoveries at Herculaneum," 58-59.

EXERCISE

Given the Works Cited (or Bibliography) entries below as the general source listing for a research paper, prepare a Notes page to include the numbered exercise items that follow the list.

Crowell, Donald. <u>Roman Frescoes</u>. New York: Westhaven Art, 1983.

Hughes, Janet. <u>Roman Mosaics and Wall Paintings</u>. 2 vols. London: Westminster, 1983.

Larson, Fred. "Roman Apartment Construction Techniques." <u>Engineering Review</u> 19 (1984): 372-95.

Merrill, Jessica. "The Oscan and Samnite Heritage at Herculaneum and Pompeii." <u>Roman Culture</u>. Ed. Caroline Stewart. New York: Shirlington, 1982. 58-74.

Mills, Michael, and Franca Cipri. "Mt. St. Helens Helps Explain A.D. 79 Eruption of Vesuvius." <u>Museum News</u> 10 Feb. 1984: 26-38.

Rocci, Antonio. "Ercolano's Volcanic Matrix Yields More Victims of Vesuvius." <u>World Science</u> ns 9 (1985): 148-53.

1. Pages 381 to 382 of Fred Larson's article.

2. Page 153 of Antonio Rocci's article.

3. Page 373 of Fred Larson's article.

4. Page 24 of Donald Crowell's book.

5. Page 63 of Jessica Merrill's essay.

6. Page 171 of Antonio Rocci's article.

7. Page 55 of volume 2 of the two-volume set by Janet Hughes.

8. Page 30 of the article by Michael Mills and Franca Cipri.

12

Other Documentation Styles

The general-purpose documentation styles detailed in the previous chapters are not used in some academic and professional fields, so you may need to learn how to format reference information in other ways. Fortunately, as Chapter 9 indicates, most documentation styles agree about the content of a specific documentation entry for an article or book; differences are primarily in format conventions. This chapter outlines two more common documentation styles: the **APA style,** used extensively in the social sciences, and the **numbered reference style,** used primarily in some of the physical sciences. In addition, at the end of the chapter is a list of style manuals you may need to consult for documentation practices within specific fields.

APA STYLE

The Formats for documentation in this portion of the chapter generally follow the third edition of the *Publication Manual of the American Psychological Association*, published by the American Psychological Association (APA). If the academic field you are writing for requires use of author-year documentation, check to see whether the APA style is acceptable or whether you need to examine a different style guide.

Like the parenthetical documentation system in Chapter 9, the APA style depends on interaction of material in two portions of your research paper:

- **General source listing.** At the end of the research paper is an alphabetized list, called *References,* of entries with full bibliographic information about each source document for the research paper.

158

- **Specific portion reference.** Within the body of the research paper, along with presentations of material from your sources, you include in parentheses a documentation reference to the specific portion(s) of the source or sources supporting your text. This parenthetical information provides readers with a cross-reference to data in the References listing so they can connect the general and specific documentation portions.

Notice the parenthetical reference in the following sample text from a research paper using APA style:

> According to one study of mental disorders among patients in nursing homes, being deprived of associations with familiar individuals and life patterns from their own homes was the primary factor in their progressive mental deterioration (Wyman, 1985, p. 54).

The **specific portion reference** is *(Wyman, 1985, p. 54). Wyman, 1985* tells readers to look for that entry in the References list. At the end of the research paper, then, is the References section, the **general source listing.** There readers would find this entry:

> Wyman, P. A. (1985). <u>The problems of aging: Mental disorders and the disintegration of the extended family</u>. New York: Schocken.

The References entry begins with the author's last name, and that name element is followed by publication year—the cross-reference data in the author-year reference in parentheses in the text. Of course, the *p. 54* in the parenthetical reference cites the specific portion of Wyman's book to which the student's paper refers.

BASIC AUTHOR-YEAR REFERENCE FORMS

Work with one name listed

When a References entry begins with only one person's name, use the last name, publication year, and page reference: (Wyman, 1985, p. 54) or (Wyman, 1985, pp. 54–56). If the name has a qualifier such as "Ed.," do not include the qualifier in the parenthetical reference.

Work with two names listed

When a References entry begins with two names, so must the parenthetical reference to it. Join the two last names with an ampersand (&): (Herman & Reynolds, 1986, p. 73).

Work with three to five names listed

The first reference in your research paper should list all the authors: (Roberts, Shields, & Newton, 1984, p. 91). Subsequent references should cite only the name listed first, followed by *et al.* in place of the other names: (Roberts et al., 1984, p. 94).

Work with six or more names listed

When a References entry begins with six or more names, for the author portion of the author-year reference use only the name listed first and *et al.* for the other authors: (Newman et al., 1983, pp. 115–17).

Multiple works listed for the same name(s) and year

When the References list shows two or more publications by the same author(s) that were published in the same year, the one listed first in References would include the letter *a* with the publication year, the one listed second would have *b* with the year, and so on. Those letter additions to the year are used in the parenthetical references as well, as in (Andrews, 1985a, p. 32) or (Andrews, 1985b, p. 89).

Citing an entire work

Writing in the social sciences frequently requires general references to works as well as the specific place references illustrated above. A textual reference to an entire work simply eliminates the page reference: (Wyman, 1985).

Streamlining author-year references

If the text names the author and/or gives the publication year, then the parenthetical reference can be shortened appropriately or eliminated altogether. Thus, the sample passage and reference shown earlier could look like this instead:

> According to Wyman's study of mental disorders among patients in nursing homes, being deprived of associations with familiar individuals and life patterns from their own homes was the primary factor in their progressive mental deterioration (1985, p. 54).

Or this:

> In his 1985 study of mental disorders among patients in nursing homes, Wyman maintains that being deprived of associations with familiar individuals and life patterns in their own homes was the primary factor in their progressive mental deterioration (p. 54).

And no parenthetical reference would appear with the following general reference to the study as a whole:

Wyman's 1985 study of mental disorders among patients in nursing homes associates stages of mental deterioration with the disintegration of the extended family.

No page reference is appropriate, and the text itself provides both author and publication year as the cross-reference to the References list, so no parenthetical reference is required in the text.

REFERENCE LIST

At the end of the paper you list all sources cited in your research paper. Arrange the entries in alphabetical order. You can use the sample at the beginning of Chapter 10 for spacing guidance for page layout (page 120); of course, change the title to "References." In addition, the information that appears in each type of source entry in Chapter 10 should be included here also. However, the style of entries from Chapter 10 would have to be modified for the APA author-year documentation system. Look at what's special about a sample References entry for a book in the APA author-year system:

Wyman, P. A. (1985). The problems of aging: Mental disorders and the disintegration of the extended family. New York: Schocken.

- Only initials appear for the author's first and middle names; this is true regardless of whether the work itself gives full name or only initials.
- The year of publication follows the author element of the entry rather than appearing at the end with the other publication information. Remember, add *a, b,* and so on, to the dates if References lists more than one work with identical author element and year.
- Only the first word of the title and subtitle are capitalized.

Following are common formats for Reference list entries for books and articles in periodicals. For other works, adapt the styles illustrated in Chapter 10 by reducing the authors' first and middle names to initials, moving the publication date to follow the author element, and altering capitalization within book and article titles.

One author

Wyman, P. A. (1985). The problems of aging: Mental disorders and the disintegration of the extended family. New York: Schocken.

Two or more authors

All authors' names are presented in reverse order (i.e., last name-first initial-middle initial).

Herman, G. R., & Reynolds, M. E. (1986). Sociopathic behavior. Washington: Steinman.

Roberts, B. A., Shields, M., & Newton, J. L. (1986). Psychopaths and prisons: Aberration and integration in a closed society. New York: Shirlington.

Editor(s)

Show "(Ed.)." or "(Eds.)." after the name element.

Stanley, H. R. (Ed.). (1985). Patterns of learning. Washington: Luke.

Journal with continuous pagination

Although the article title follows the capitalization rules above, capitalize all major words in the journal title. Underline (or italicize) the journal title, but present the article title without either underlining or quotation marks. The volume number, underlined (or italicized), follows the journal title. Do not use "p." or "pp." with the inclusive page references for journal articles.

Johnston, M. (1984). Growing up in prison: Juvenile learning behind bars. Journal of Social Behavior, 15, 323-46.

Journal with issues paged independently

Include the volume number with underlining (italics), followed by the issue number in parentheses but without underlining.

Evangelist, B. A., & Worthington, B. (1985). Criminal sexual psychopaths. Prison Psychology, 21 (5), 33-49.

Magazine

Instead of volume and/or issue, include month(s) of publication with the year. For magazine and newspaper articles, use "p." or "pp." with the inclusive pagination.

Ellsworth, P. S. (1985, February). Depression among housewives. Social Issues Today, pp. 27-36.

Newspaper

If the article shows the author, begin with the author's last name, as in the first sample below. If no author is given, begin with the article title, as in the second sample. The date element includes the full date of publication.

Braddy, R. J. (1985, November 23). Addictions in the military services. Washington Post, pp. A11-A13.

Drugs and the army. (1985, October 12). Washington Post, p. B9.

APA STYLE SAMPLE

The following excerpt from an informative research paper on "Down's syndrome" demonstrates use of APA style. The portion on the following pages follows sections on the genetic causes of Down's syndrome (or Mongolism) and the clinical features of the condition and precedes a section on overall prognosis and life expectancy. The reference list that follows the excerpt is for the entire research paper, not just the extracted portion.

A Notice the author and year are in parentheses and that the period for the sentence follows the parentheses.

B Here the author is already given in the text, so it need not be repeated in the parenthetical citation. Always include the page numbers for quotations.

C These paraphrases do not need parenthetical citations: the source and date are given in the text. Notice the introduction to the paraphrase—"A 1965 U.S. Department of . . . " shows clearly where the paraphrasing begins. The layout—paragraphs set off from the text—shows clearly where the paraphrasing takes place and ends.

Training and Education

Of the more than 100 indications of Down's syndrome, mental retardation predominates (Robinson, 1972). While this retardation ranges from mild to severe, the majority of individuals with Down's syndrome are capable of being trained to provide some of their own care, requiring only moderate supervision, and some individuals can be educated at the elementary school level.

Barnett (1972, p. 897) provides the following assessment of the degrees of mental retardation associated with the Down's condition: "The intelligence of patients with Down's syndrome is variable and follows a bell-shaped curve, with a median IQ of 40 to 50 in home-reared children, and an overall range of 20 to 70." Berkow (1982, p. 1924) marks the mean IQ at "about 50." In general, then, the majority of individuals with Down's syndrome can be expected to show mental retardation in the mild to moderate range.

A 1965 U.S. Department of Health, Education, and Welfare basic reference publication, relating degrees of mental retardation to developmental potential, suggests the upper limits of achievement for individuals with Down's syndrome:

Severely retarded persons (IQ 20-35) in the 0 to 5 age range are likely to possess only minimal speech and communication ability and are unlikely to learn to care for themselves. From age 6 to 20, they probably can talk or otherwise learn to communicate and can be trained in basic health habits,

given systematic training. In the adult years (age 21+) they are likely to be able to care for themselves somewhat under close supervision, and probably will not hurt themselves as long as they are supervised.

Moderately retarded persons (IQ 35-50) in the 0 to 5 age range can either talk or learn to communicate and particularly benefit from training in self-care skills; however, they are likely to have difficulties adjusting to social norms. They can be trained to require only moderate supervision. From age 6 to 20 they can learn social and job skills but academically are unlikely to exceed the second grade level. As adults they can cope with semi-skilled or less challenging work in a sheltered workshop environment, yet are likely to need supervision to deal with mild stress.

Mildly retarded persons (IQ 50–70) in the 0 to 5 age range are capable of developing communication and social skills. At this age, in fact, many may not appear different from "normal" children. By late adolescence, they may reach a grade six equivalence academically and can be trained to conform to social norms in public. Adults usually are capable of working at simple, repetitive jobs in the community, although they are likely to need supervision if faced with moderate to severe stress.

Authorities warn that few individuals with Down's syndrome exceed the development of an average child aged 5 to 7 (Marlow, 1969). Still, given that the majority can

D   Notice in this collection of quotations that the reader benefits from the extra information—names, dates—that superscript notes in the *MLA* system don't provide as readily.

be expected to be mildly or moderately retarded, they have the potential for training and in some cases for elementary education. Thus, as Cornwell (1985) notes, they "can develop their full potential within the limits of their disability."

Although the severely retarded probably need to be cared for in institutions or special foster homes, moderately and mildly retarded individuals with Down's syndrome appear to profit from home rearing and con-

D   trolled exposure to the community. "Most experts recommend that less seriously handicapped children live at home. Scientific studies show that, in general, children reared at home have a higher IQ and usually achieve more than those raised in institutions" (Cornwell, 1985). As another source puts it: "Good care, affectionate handling, and education to the limit of their capabilities render many of these children tractable, pleasant, and able to perform simple but useful tasks" (Ziai, Janeway, & Cooke, 1969, p. 77). Particularly important for the development of the individual with Down's syndrome is the education of the parents. Marlow (1969) argues that parents have difficulty understanding the Down's child's condition and capabilities; the parents, therefore, need professional counseling to understand and accept not only the limitations of their child but also the child's capabilities. The community also affects the development of Down's individuals. As Cornwell (1985) indicates, some communities provide special classes in public schools and special workshops that employ adults with Down's syndrome. Of course, lack of community acceptance ultimately limits development potential; Barnett (1972, p. 899) cautions: "Very few, if any, become independent in the community. Their cosmetic defect adds to their problem in being accepted, even if their IQ permits them to compete vocationally."

References

Barnett, H. L. (Ed.). (1972). Pediatrics. 15th ed. New York: Appleton.

Berkow, R. (Ed.). (1982). The Merck manual of diagnosis and therapy. 14th ed. Rahway, NJ: Merck.

Cornwell, A. C. (1985). Down's syndrome. In The world book encyclopedia. Chicago: World Book.

Harvey, A. M., Johns, R. J., McKusick, V. A., Owens, A. H., & Ross, R. S. (1980). The principles and practice of medicine. 20th ed. New York: Appleton.

Marlow, D. R. (1969). Textbook of pediatric nursing. 3rd ed. Philadelphia: Saunders.

Robinson, L. (1972). Psychiatric nursing as a human experience. Philadelphia: Saunders.

Taber, C. W. (1965). Taber's cyclopedic medical dictionary. 10th ed. Philadelphia: Davis.

United States. Dept. of Health, Education, and Welfare. (1965). An introduction to mental retardation: Problems, plans and programs. Washington: GPO.

Ziai, M., Janeway, C. A., & Cooke, R. E. (Eds.). (1969). Pediatrics. Boston: Little.

NUMBERED REFERENCE STYLE

In a numbered reference style the works in the general source listing at the end of the research paper are numbered sequentially. References in parentheses within the text of the paper give the number of the work in the source listing and the specific page reference, for example "(7:54)":

> According to one study of mental disorders among patients in nursing homes, being deprived of associations with familiar individuals and life patterns from their own homes was the primary factor in their progressive mental deterioration (7:54).

Or, for a generalized reference to the work as a whole, only the number of the work in the source listing, for example "(7)":

> Wyman's study associates stages of mental deterioration with the disintegration of the extended family (7).

Call the general source listing "Works Cited," "References," or "List of References." Works may be listed in alphabetical order or in the order in which they are first cited in the research paper's text.

NUMBERED REFERENCE STYLE SAMPLE

The following pages repeat the excerpt from the research paper about Down's syndrome—but this time documentation follows the numbered reference style. As before, the reference list is for the entire research paper. For this sample the sources were listed in alphabetical order before they were numbered.

A   The 6 tells you this citation is the sixth source on the References page; the 334 tells you the paraphrased material came from page 334 of that source.

B   For a paraphrase you need give only the number of the source— not necessarily the page numbers.

Training and Education

A Of the more than 100 indications of Down's syndrome, mental retardation predominates (6:334). While this retardation ranges from mild to severe, the majority of individuals with Down's syndrome are capable of being trained to provide some of their own care, requiring only moderate supervision, and some individuals can be educated at the elementary school level.

Barnett provides the following assessment of the degrees of mental retardation associated with the Down's condition: "The intelligence of patients with Down's syndrome is variable and follows a bell-shaped curve, with a median IQ of 40 to 50 in home-reared children, and an overall range of 20 to 70" (1:897). Berkow marks the mean IQ at "about 50" (2:1924). In general, then, the majority of individuals with Down's syndrome can be expected to show mental retardation in the mild to moderate range.

A U.S. Department of Health, Education, and Welfare basic reference publication (8), relating degrees of mental retardation to developmental potential, suggests the upper limits of achievement for individuals with Down's syndrome:

> Severely retarded persons (IQ 20-35) in the 0 to 5 age range are likely to possess only minimal speech and communication ability and are unlikely to learn to care for themselves. From age 6 to 20, they probably can talk or otherwise learn to communicate and can be trained in basic health habits, given systematic training. In the adult years (age 21 +) they are likely to be able to care for them-

selves somewhat under close supervision, and likely won't hurt themselves so long as they are supervised.

Moderately retarded persons (IQ 35-50) in the 0 to 5 age range can either talk or learn to communicate and particularly benefit from training in self-care skills; however, they are likely to have difficulties adjusting to social norms. They can be trained to require only moderate supervision. From age 6 to 20 they can learn social and job skills but academically are unlikely to exceed the second grade level. As adults they can cope with semi-skilled or less challenging work in a sheltered workshop environment, yet are likely to need supervision to deal with mild stress.

Mildly retarded persons (IQ 50-70) in the 0 to 5 age range are capable of developing communication and social skills. At this age, in fact, many may not appear different from "normal" children. By late adolescence, they may reach a grade six equivalence academically and can be trained to conform to social norms in public. Adults usually are capable of working at simple, repetitive jobs in the community, although they are likely to need supervision if faced with moderate to severe stress. Authorities warn that few individuals with Down's syndrome exceed the development of an average child aged 5 to 7 (5:221). Still, given that the majority can be expected to be mildly or moderately retarded, they have the potential for training and in some cases for elementary education. Thus, as Cornwell notes, they "can develop their full potential within the limits of their disability" (3).

Although the severely retarded probably need to be cared for in institutions or special foster homes, moderately and mildly retarded individuals with Down's syndrome appear to profit from home rearing and controlled exposure to the community. "Most experts recommend that less seriously handicapped children live at home. Scientific studies show that, in general, children reared at home have a higher IQ and usually achieve more than those raised in institutions" (3). As another source puts it: "Good care, affectionate handling, and education to the limit of their capabilities render many of these children tractable, pleasant, and able to perform simple but useful tasks" (9:77). Particularly important for the development of the individual with Down's syndrome is the education of the parents. Marlow argues that parents have difficulty understanding the Down's child's condition and capabilities; the parents, therefore, need professional counseling to understand and accept not only the limitations of their child but also the child's capabilities (5:221). The community also affects the development of Down's individuals. As Cornwell indicates, some communities provide special classes in public schools and special workshops that employ adults with Down's syndrome (3). Of course, lack of community acceptance ultimately limits development potential; Barnett cautions: "Very few, if any, become independent in the community. Their cosmetic defect adds to their problem in being accepted, even if their IQ permits them to compete vocationally" (1:899).

References

1. Barnett, H. L. (Ed.). (1972). <u>Pediatrics</u>. 15th ed. New York: Appleton.
2. Berkow, R. (Ed.). (1982). <u>The Merck manual of diagnosis and therapy</u>. 14th ed. Rahway, NJ: Merck.
3. Cornwell, A. C. (1985). Down's syndrome. In <u>The world book encyclopedia</u>. Chicago: World Book.
4. Harvey, A. M., Johns, R. J., McKusick, V. A., Owens, A. H., & Ross, R. S. (1980). <u>The principles and practice of medicine</u>. 20th ed. New York: Appleton.
5. Marlow, D. R. (1969). <u>Textbook of pediatric nursing</u>. 3rd ed. Philadelphia: Saunders.
6. Robinson, L. (1972). <u>Psychiatric nursing as a human experience</u>. Philadelphia: Saunders.
7. Taber, C. W. (1965). <u>Taber's cyclopedic medical dictionary</u>. 10th ed. Philadelphia: Davis.
8. United States. Dept. of Health, Education, and Welfare. (1965). <u>An introduction to mental retardation: Problems, plans and programs</u>. Washington: GPO.
9. Ziai, M., Janeway, C. A., & Cooke, R. E. (Eds.). (1969). <u>Pediatrics</u>. Boston: Little.

OTHER DOCUMENTATION STYLE GUIDES

Biology   Council of Biology Editors. Style Manual Committee. *CBE Style Manual: A Guide for Authors, Editors, and Publishers in the Biological Sciences.* 5th ed. Bethesda: Council of Biology Editors, 1983.

Chemistry   American Chemical Society. *Handbook for Authors of Papers in American Chemical Society Publications.* Washington: American Chemical Soc., 1978.

Geology   United States. Geological Survey. *Suggestions to Authors of the Reports of the United States Geological Survey.* 6th ed. Washington: GPO, 1978.

Linguistics   Linguistic Society of America. *LSA Bulletin*, Dec. issue, annually.

Mathematics	American Mathematical Society. *A Manual for Authors of Mathematical Papers.* 7th ed. Providence: American Mathematical Soc., 1980.
Medicine	International Steering Committee of Medical Editors. "Uniform Requirements for Manuscripts Submitted to Biomedical Journals." *Annals of Internal Medicine* 90 (Jan. 1979): 95-99.
Physics	American Institute of Physics. Publications Board. *Style Manual for Guidance in the Preparation of Papers.* 3rd ed. New York: American Inst. of Physics, 1978.
Psychology	American Psychological Association. *Publication Manual of the American Psychological Association.* 3rd ed. Washington: American Psychological Assn., 1983.

13   Illustrations

When you're leafing through a book or journal, isn't your attention drawn almost automatically to the illustrations? Yet, except for technical subjects, few students think of using illustrations in their papers. In the paper you're writing, could you make something clearer or more interesting by illustrating it? A good illustration could be one of the high points of your paper. Of course, don't put in a picture of a mountain range just because you're writing about mountain climbing; that will not help the reader understand your paper. But do use illustrations to clarify or emphasize important points.

KINDS OF ILLUSTRATIONS

There are two kinds of illustrations: tables and figures. A *table* lists information in rows and columns—horizontally, vertically, or both. A *figure* is any illustration that isn't a table, such as a graph, drawing, photograph, or diagram. Also, a combination of table and figure—for example, columnar data combined with a graph—is a figure.

When you number your illustrations, number them consecutively by kind (Table 1, Table 2, and so on; and Figure 1, Figure 2, and so on).

TABLES

There are numerous ways to present information in a table, depending on the complexity of the data you have to tabulate. Always, however, your aim should be to arrange the information so it is easy to understand. Thus, the layout should be simple, not showy. The following is a suggested format for fitting the table into the text of the paper.

- *Quadruple-space between the text and the table number and descriptive title.*

- *Center the table number and descriptive title above the table.*
- *If your table presents material gained from research, place the appropriate parenthetical reference or footnote number at the end of the descriptive title.* (The sample below illustrates a parenthetical reference; a footnote, of course, would go in the same place.)
- *With black ink or pencil, neatly draw a box around the table.* (This step highlights the information, further setting it apart from the text. You may find other ways you prefer to fulfill that purpose, but whatever method you use, make it neat and keep it simple.)
- *Quadruple-space between the bottom of the table and the paper's text.*

Here's a sample table, one that might appear in a paper discussing technical mountaineering in the Garden of the Gods, Colorado:

Table 2. Popular Technical Rock Climbs in the Garden of the Gods (Stanley 127).

Climb	Successful Ascents in 1980
Anaconda	3
Amazing Grace	5
Borderline	11
Max's Mayhem	12
Borghoff's Blunder	84
Dust to Dust	86
Henry the Pig	94
Monster	105
Snuggles	117
Lower Fingertip Traverse	176
Potholes	253

FIGURES

Here is a suggested format for integrating figures with your paper:

- *Quadruple-space from the text to the top of the figure.*
- *Double-space from the bottom of the figure to the figure number and descriptive title.*
- *If appropriate, place a parenthetical reference or footnote number at the end of the descriptive title.* (Again, the sample following illustrates a parenthetical reference.)

• *Quadruple-space from the figure number and descriptive title to the text of your paper.*

The following is a sample figure—in this case, a graph presenting data to support the point that most climbing in the Garden of the Gods takes place in the spring and fall:

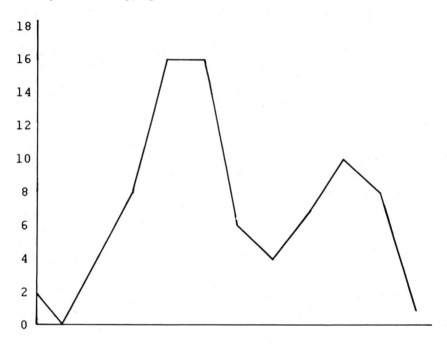

Jan Feb Mar Apr May Jun Jul Aug Sep Oct Nov Dec

**Figure   1.   Frequency   of   Successful   Ascents
of Borghoff's Blunder in 1980[6]**

(Note: In this graph the meanings of the horizontal and vertical axes are obvious, so labels such as "Months" and "Number of Successful Ascents" are unnecessary. However, you should label the axes if readers might have difficulty understanding what the units stand for.)

SUCCESSFUL ILLUSTRATIONS

There's more to a successful illustration than following these formats for fitting the material onto the page. Here are some tips:

• *Don't cramp the illustration.* Make the illustration large enough that the information is easy to see. Also, allow enough space on the page so that the illustration doesn't seem jammed into your paper. You'll have to plan ahead when you type—maybe even type a draft on a sheet of scratch paper.

- *Keep the illustration uncluttered.* Don't try to do so many things at once that an illustration seems busy. Three or four simple, uncluttered visuals will be much more effective than one that attempts everything.

- *Label the illustration clearly.* A good illustration has the potential to stand alone—independent of the text of the paper. Of course, an illustration is related to the text: The illustration supports a point in the paper, so the text helps explain the illustration, and vice versa. Nevertheless, readers shouldn't need to look back and forth to understand either the text or the illustration. Therefore, don't depend on the text to explain the markings on your illustration; instead, label as necessary so that the illustration can be independent. At the same time, as the sample figure in this chapter shows, you don't need to clutter the illustration with unnecessary labels.

- *Refer to the illustration in the text and explain the point it makes.* You wouldn't bother to illustrate a point if it weren't important, so be sure to do two things: Make the point in the text of your paper—not just in the illustration; and, while you're making the point in your text, refer the reader to the illustration.

- *Place the illustration close to where you mention it.* But don't put the illustration before the place you discuss it. If necessary, use a facing page—an extra, unnumbered page that would be the left page if you opened your paper like a book. That way, both the illustration and the discussion face the reader at the same time.

- *Be neat.* Type all labels you can and use a straightedge wherever possible.

- *Be imaginative.* A vivid presentation can create for the reader that picture that substitutes for many words. Consider using colors for contrast in figures (but it you plan to copy the paper, remember that most copying machines reproduce colors only as shades of gray). And although the illustration shouldn't be flashy, it should be pleasing to look at, perhaps even decorative.

14

Special Considerations for the Technical Paper

Technical writing differs from other kinds of research writing in several key ways:

Relatively specific and narrow audience

Knowing who will read a technical report helps you determine the purpose of the report, the amount of technical detail to include, and the kind of language to use. For example, a proposal to a city council for a nature shelter will have a different purpose, detail, and language from a bid specification for contractors to build the shelter. Despite these differences, both are technical kinds of writing.

Extensive use of numbers and technical details

Numbers are the basic language of the technical writer. Technical writing uses such details as length, width, volume, extent of motion, and formulas to help describe, clarify, and explain. This chapter gives some guidelines for presenting numbers in your paper.

Frequent use of illustrations

Illustrations can appear in any type of research paper, but they appear very frequently in technical writing. Any graphic means—photographs, equations, graphs, drawings, charts—will help readers understand the written part of the technical paper. As with other kinds of writing, however, a good technical paper uses visual aids to support the words in the text, never to take their place. The guidance in Chapter 13 for presenting illustrations in research papers also applies to technical papers.

Special forms of documenation

Some scientific disciplines require special documentation forms. See Chapter 12 for systems common in some of the social and physical sciences. (Or you may be able to use one of the general-purpose documentation systems discussed in Chapters 9 through 11.)

Highly standardized formats

Although minor differences occur among industries and scientific disciplines, fairly standard formats for technical reports make the technical writer's (and reader's) job a bit easier. This chapter discusses a basic format and illustrates the preliminary pages of a sample technical report.

EXPRESSION

Write with active verbs as often as you can. Sometimes, of course, passive verbs are appropriate because the actor is either unknown or unimportant. Otherwise, use active verbs to keep your technical writing straightforward. And there is no law against using the personal *I* rather than the impersonal phrase "it was found by this researcher." Use personal pronouns when you can do so without drawing inappropriate attention to yourself. The idea that used to be common—the absolute, cold impersonality of science and its investigators—has begun to give way to a realistic recognition that people do the investigating and that we ought to acknowledge that fact in our writing. The best technical writing blends the technical and the active, personal kinds of expression.

NUMBERS

Because technical papers usually involve extensive use of numbers, you need to adopt a consistent style for writing numbers as figures and as words. Here is one workable system:

- Generally write numbers *10* and above as figures and those below *10* as words, with these exceptions:
  In tables, write all numbers as figures.
  If two or more numbers occur within a sentence, write all of them as figures if any of them is *10* or greater (or all as words if each is less than *10*).
  Write as figures all numbers of measurement (time, linear or volume measure, percentage, proportion, and so forth).
- For readability, when numbers in the millions and billions occur

in a sentence in your paper, use a combination of figures and words: 2 million, 15 billion, and so on. However, use only figures in tables.

- No matter what the size of the number, never begin a sentence with a figure. Of course, to keep from writing out a long number in words, you can recast your sentence so that it doesn't open with a number.

HEADINGS

You've probably noticed that we use headings (or captions) in this book to mark key divisions within chapters. Headings help us keep our ideas straight, serving as a guide or outline. That's how you should use them in technical papers, too. Help your reader see where you're going, but don't use headings to take the place of transitions. In fact, it's a good idea to add headings only after you've written a draft or two of the paper. That way the paper will hold together without them. Use the kind of short, key-word captions we've used. The major and support topics from an outline of the paper sometimes make useful headings.

To help break down complex ideas into several smaller ones, you probably will need at least three levels of headings. That's easy in books because printers have the flexibility of different sizes and styles of typefaces. Still, headings are possible in typing, too. Here's one way to show three levels of headings in typewritten material:

FIRST-ORDER HEADING

Put the heading all in capital letters, aligned with the left margin and on a line by itself without punctuation.

Second-Order Heading

Also align second-order headings with the left margin. Underline each heading and give it a line by itself. However, capitalize only the first letter of each key word, as you would in the title of a book or article (see rules for capitalization in titles on page 140).

Third-Order Heading. Capitalize as with second-order headings, but indent third-order headings as you would the beginning of a paragraph. Underline them and punctuate them with periods; then begin your text on the same line, as we do here.

BASIC PARTS OF A TECHNICAL PAPER

Some parts of a technical paper are like those you've written for other research papers. Both kinds require an introduction, a body, and a conclusion of some sort. We'll discuss the specific requirements for a technical paper in the rest of this chapter.

TITLE PAGE

Use the same kind of title page as for other research papers. The sample title page in Chapter 7 and the one illustrated at the end of this chapter are good models to follow.

TABLE OF CONTENTS

As the sample Table of Contents at the end of this chapter shows, you should list the major divisions of your paper—the preliminary matter of the paper (minus the title page and the Table of Contents itself); the parts of the body of the paper that are marked by headings; References, List of References, or Notes and Works Cited, as appropriate; and the appendixes. Because the portion of the table of contents that represents the body of the paper corresponds to an outline, there's seldom a need to submit an outline, also, for a technical research paper.

LIST OF ILLUSTRATIONS

In a technical paper, provide a list of illustrations whenever you have three or more illustrations. List them on a separate page immediately following the Table of Contents. You will find a sample at the end of this chapter.

LIST OF SYMBOLS AND DEFINITIONS

Opinions differ on the value of a List of Symbols and Definitions in a technical paper. You always must beware of seeming to write in a code that only you and a few special readers can understand. Some instructors of technical writing fear that including a list of symbols and definitions at the beginning of a paper encourages you to write in such a code; that is, having provided a list for translation, you may no longer feel the need to explain yourself in your paper.

That needn't be the case, however. You can explain terms as you use them in your paper and still provide a list at the front as a handy reference for your readers. The sample preliminary pages at the end of this chapter include a List of Symbols and Definitions; notice, though, that the sample abstract following the list also explains the symbols as they occur in the writing.

ABSTRACT

An abstract is a brief summary of a piece of writing. We talked about volumes of abstracts as library research tools in Chapter 3, but now you must write an abstract for your own paper. Obviously you can't write an abstract to summarize the paper until after you've written the rest of the paper. So although the abstract is part of the preliminary matter of your paper, it's one of the last things you write. You may be asked to write either a descriptive or an informative abstract; descriptive abstracts are most common in library reference tools, but informative abstracts are preferable when an abstract accompanies the paper itself.

Descriptive abstract

This kind of abstract describes the paper itself; it tells readers what is covered in the study. That is, a descriptive abstract discusses the *report* but not the *subject:* we still have to read the report to find out what the author has to say about the subject. A descriptive abstract, then, usually is useful only for alerting readers that the report contains something of interest to them.

Informative abstract

This kind of abstract—the one we recommend—is more useful and complete. The sample preliminary pages at the end of this chapter contain an informative abstract you can use as a model. An informative abstract does more than merely name the topics in a report; it tells the key ideas, summarizes basic facts, and reports the major conclusions or decisions. Because it summarizes the report, an informative abstract eliminates the need for a special section that otherwise might be required before the report is submitted to a busy executive.

INTRODUCTION

Following the abstract comes the report, beginning with an introduction. Its purpose in a technical paper is somewhat different from that described in Chapter 5 for other research papers. Because technical writing fulfills a business function, there's less need to motivate readers; instead, describing the purpose and problem of a paper is sufficient motivation since scientists and executives already are interested in what the technical writer has to report.

Purpose

The purpose division of the introduction is a simple statement of the function of the report itself. While we have not included an entire sample technical paper, here is the purpose statement that accompanies the preliminary pages illustrated at the end of this chapter:

> **This report examines whether the Cambridge Utilities Corporation should use standard head-loss coefficients for predicting fluid pressure changes through pipe fittings or should conduct an extended experiment to determine specific coefficients for its products.**

Problem

This division outlines the problem that led to the report.

Scope

This division of the introduction explains what the report contains by showing how the report is put together. That is, it summarizes briefly the major elements of the body of the report to alert the readers to the organization of the rest of the paper. In addition, the scope section may include a discussion of the limitations of the report—a statement of what the report does not include and an explanation of why those things don't matter.

BODY

The contents of the body of a technical paper vary greatly with the purpose of the report. To reduce the complexity of the technical material, break it into units your readers can easily comprehend, and label the units with headings (or captions) like those we described earlier.

In addition, you'll have to consider where you want to present complex technical details. Sometimes the technical data are the body of the paper. More often, however, some of the more complex material can be filtered out and placed in supporting appendixes at the back of the report. Because you frequently must write for an audience made up both of technically prepared individuals and of managers without that same technical background, we recommend that you put such details as extensive calculations, computer printouts, and derivations of formulas in appendixes at the end of the paper. Putting the data there allows you and your readers to concentrate on the discussion, but technical readers also will have all the material available to examine the strength of your findings and conclusions.

Less complex supporting material—particularly illustrations—directly pertinent to the text should appear in the text. Include illustrations within the text, or if an illustration requires a full page, attach it to the back of the preceding page so that it faces the text that refers to it.

CONCLUSIONS

Make certain that the conclusions are clear and are drawn from the evidence you present, just as in other kinds of writing.

RECOMMENDATIONS

If the paper is being written to suggest the resolution of a question, you *must* include a recommendations section. It, too, should be stated clearly so that there is no mistake about what you recommend.

DOCUMENTATION

Following the conclusions and/or recommendations comes the documentation of your sources—References, List of References, or Notes and Works Cited, as appropriate.

APPENDIXES

Some technical papers will have no appendixes, others as many as 20 or more. The sample Table of Contents following lists five appendixes, and their titles suggest the types of material appropriate for this portion of a technical paper.

SAMPLE PRELIMINARY PAGES

On the next few pages you'll find samples of the preliminary parts of a technical paper—a title page, a Table of Contents, a List of Illustrations, a List of Symbols and Definitions, and an informative abstract. They came from an excellent paper written by one of our students, Joseph L. Smith, who wrote the paper as if he had worked on a practical problem in industry. We have not included the whole paper, but these preliminary pages will tell you a lot about writing technical papers.

DETERMINING HEAD-LOSS COEFFICIENTS

by

Joseph L. Smith

for

Mr. William F. McNary
Vice President, Cambridge Utilities Corporation
January 2, 1981

Table of Contents

List of Illustrations

List of Symbols and Definitions

Symbol	Definition	Units
A	Pipe cross sectional area	m^2
g	Acceleration due to gravity	m/s^2
H	Mercury column height in manometers 1 through 6	m
H_1	Mercury column height in manometer 1	m
h_L	Head loss	m
K_L	Head-loss coefficient	none
$\dot{m}$	Flow rate	kg/s
V	Fluid velocity	m/s
ΔP	Pressure change	Pa
γ_{ok}	Weight density of oil-kerosene	N/m^3
γ_{Hg}	Weight density of mercury	N/m^3

v

195

Abstract

To satisfy consumer needs, the Cambridge Utilities Corporation (CUC) must determine head-loss coefficients for its angle valves, globe valves, gate valves, 90-degree elbows, 45-degree elbows, and plugged-tee pipe fittings. Head-loss coefficients (K_L values) make it easier to predict pressure changes that occur when a fluid flows through a pipe fitting. Standard K_L values for common pipe fittings are known already:

Type	K_L
angle valve	2.0
90-degree elbow	0.3
45-degree elbow	0.2
plugged tee	0.9
gate valve	0.1
globe valve	10.0

The CUC must determine whether these standard K_L values can be used for its fittings or if a specific determination of the values for its fittings is needed.

The pressure change across a pipe fitting (ΔP) is related to K_L values in this way:

$$K_L = 2g\Delta P/(V^2\gamma)$$

where

g = acceleration due to gravity, m/s^2

v = fluid velocity, m/s

γ = weight density of the fluid, N/m^3

Experimental data obtained for the CUC's fittings when g, ΔP, V, and γ were known yielded these results:

Type	K_L
angle valve	3.6
90-degree elbow	0.5
45-degree elbow	0.3
plugged tee	0.9
gate valve	0.01
globe valve	8.6

These data indicate that standard K_L values deviate too much from the CUC's K_L values to use the standard for predicting pressure changes. The CUC must conduct an extended experimental determination of K_L unique to its fittings.

vi

Appendix: Annotated List of Sources by Academic Discipline

This appendix lists some helpful sources to start you on your research. Arranged by academic disciplines, the lists are not exhaustive in any sense—but they do show basic research works, the kinds your college library is likely to have, for the fields covered. Here are the types of works included, although not every type is given for every field:

- For most disciplines you'll find a *bibliography* or *index* to lead you to periodicals and books about the specific topic you're working on.
- Often you'll find an *abstract*, especially for large or technical disciplines.
- When one is available, you'll see an introductory *guide to literature* for a field; this type of reference work explains the types of material available in the field and how the information is organized in libraries. A guide of this type can save you time because it shows how to conduct research in its particular discipline.
- For most disciplines you'll find *journals* or *magazines* important for the field.
- Sometimes you'll see a *dictionary* or *encyclopedia* for a particular subject. Because they explain the words and ideas peculiar to their disciplines, these, too, can be important research tools.

GENERAL RESEARCH WORKS

Read Chapter 3 for its discussion of general research tools. Though not dedicated specifically to a single academic discipline, the general indexes and bibliographies should be used along with the more specific tools

197

you'll find listed in this appendix. Note particularly the discussion in Chapter 3 of the *Bibliographic Index,* which can lead you to bibliographies for your subject, especially current bibliographies that might not appear in reference works a few years old.

In addition, if your library doesn't have the books we list for your subject or if you're writing on a subject we don't cover, try the following two sources for leads:

Besterman, Theodore. *A World Bibliography of Bibliographies.* 4th ed. 5 vols. Lausanne: Societas Bibliographica, 1965–66.
A useful, basic research source that lists separately published bibliographies on an international range of subjects and authors. Use it to find bibliographies on your subject.

Sheehy, Eugene P. *Guide to Reference Works.* 9th ed. Chicago: American Library Association, 1973.
This is a book librarians use to select the best reference works on nearly every major and most minor subjects. Use it as a shortcut to find the best books to help you with your topic.

Ulrich's International Periodicals Directory. New York: R. R. Bowker.
This is a comprehensive guide to periodicals—a list of all current periodicals, foreign and domestic.

SUGGESTIONS

Don't forget to check listings under major subjects that might be related to yours. If you're writing a paper in physics, you might find some help under mathematics. Or a paper in social science might be strengthened with information from sources listed under history. In other words, a good researcher must be imaginative and resourceful. Part of that resourcefulness includes knowing how to use the particular reference tool you need. So a final suggestion here is to take the brief time needed to see what the work covers, how it's organized, and what abbreviations and codes it uses. Doing so at the start will save you from wasting time as you look for information.

AERONAUTICS (SEE ALSO SCIENCE, GENERAL)

AIAA Student Journal. 1963–. (Quarterly)
This journal will appeal to student engineers and those who seek articles dealing with philosophical, historical, or practical concerns of aeronautics.

Aerospace Historian. 1954–. (Quarterly)
This journal covers primarily the history of the world's air forces and the application of air power in war.

Aviation Week and Space Technology. 1916–. (Weekly)
   The standard magazine in the field, it is reliable, accurate, and up to date in a rapidly changing world.

International Aerospace Abstracts. 1961–. (Monthly)
   Reports on published material in aeronautics and astronautics. It supplements the next entry, *STAR*.

U.S. National Aeronautics and Space Administration. *Scientific and Technical Aerospace Reports.* 1963–. (Semimonthly)
   Covers reports usually not widely published, such as those by a governmental agency or a defense contractor. See a librarian for help using *STAR*, as it's called.

AGRICULTURE (SEE ALSO BIOLOGY)

Agricultural History. 1927–. (Quarterly)
   Although it emphasizes U.S. agricultural developments, it does include world agricultural activity.

Biological and Agricultural Index: A Cumulative Subject Index to Periodicals in the Fields of Biology, Agriculture, and Related Sciences. 1964–.
   This helpful listing gives you access to materials related to agriculture.

Blanchard, Joy R., and Harold Ostvold. *Literature of Agricultural Research.* Berkeley: Univ. of California Press, 1958.
   Though partly outdated, this guide is still reliable.

U.S. National Agricultural Library. *Bibliography of Agriculture.* 1942–. (Monthly)
   A classified listing of current publications, including those produced by the Department of Agriculture.

ANTHROPOLOGY (SEE ALSO SOCIAL SCIENCE)

Abstracts in Anthropology. 1970–. (Quarterly)
   Provides abstracts from more than 300 journals, including those dealing with archaeology, ethnology, linguistics, and physical anthropology.

American Anthropologist. 1888–. (Quarterly)
   This is the major American periodical in the field; it normally carries several major articles plus useful book reviews.

Current Anthropology. 1960–. (Five issues yearly)
   Provides an exchange of ideas and reports of new trends in the field. Usually has an original article with accompanying response or com-

ment by other specialists. Useful for any student, not just the specialist.

Honigman, John J. *Handbook of Social and Cultural Anthropology.* Chicago: Rand McNally, 1973.
A review of research in the branches of anthropology, this volume also includes bibliographies and a useful subject index.

International Bibliography of Social and Cultural Anthropology. 1958–. (Annual)
Sponsored by UNESCO, it covers articles in many languages and is indexed by both author and subject.

ART

Art Bulletin. 1912–. (Quarterly)
For members of the College Art Association, this journal presents serious, learned articles on history, collections, and artists.

Art in America. 1913–. (Monthly)
A general art magazine dealing with the visual arts, largely contemporary ones.

Art Index. 1930–. (Quarterly)
An author and subject index to articles and books in all fields of the fine arts.

Myers, Bernard S., ed. *McGraw-Hill Dictionary of Art.* 5 vols. New York: McGraw-Hill, 1969.
The starting place, this standard work covers art, artists, styles, periods, and terms. Useful bibliographies, too.

ASTRONOMY (SEE ALSO SCIENCE, GENERAL)

Kemp, D. Alasdair. *Astronomy and Astrophysics: A Bibliographical Guide.* Hamden, Conn.: Archon Books, 1970.
A guide to the literature, this comprehensive volume evaluates the major books and articles on astronomy.

Rudaux, Lucien, and G. de Vancouleurs. *Larousse Encyclopedia of Astronomy.* New York: Prometheus, 1959.
Written primarily for the layman, this encyclopedia has profuse and useful illustrations.

Sky and Telescope. 1941–. (Monthly)
Includes popular and technical articles, many illustrations, and reviews.

BIOLOGY (SEE ALSO AGRICULTURE)

Abercrombie, Michael, and others. *A Dictionary of Biology*. Baltimore: Penguin, 1966.
A basic dictionary for students and laymen.

American Naturalist. 1867–. (Monthly)
Biological studies of flora and fauna with significant articles.

Biological Abstracts. 1926–. (Semimonthly)
Covers more than 5,000 periodicals. This is the basic abstract source for biology.

Biological and Agricultural Index. 1964–. (Monthly)
Abstracts in biology, agriculture, and related sciences.

Biology Digest 1974–. (Monthly)
Covers about 350 journals and provides about 500 abstracts per issue. Especially aimed at advanced high school and college students.

Bioscience. 1951–. (11/year)
This periodical for the nonspecialist covers biology, medicine, and agriculture. Well written and accessible to general students in the fields.

Bottle, Robert T., and H. V. Wyatt. *The Use of Biological Literature*. Hamden, Conn.: Archon Books, 1971.
Describes primary sources in biology and ways to find them.

Gray, Peter. *The Encyclopedia of the Biological Sciences*. New York: Van Nostrand Reinhold, 1970.
Articles for laymen and students cover the field. Helpful bibliographies.

BUSINESS (SEE ALSO ECONOMICS AND SOCIAL SCIENCE)

Ammer, Christine, and Dean S. Ammer. *Dictionary of Business and Economics*. New York: Free Press, 1984.
Defines and illustrates key words and phrases describing contemporary business practices.

Business Periodicals Index. 1958–. (Monthly)
Covers more than 200 periodicals in every field of business and management. Especially good for recent events.

Business Week. 1929–. (Weekly)
A standard, objective, general business magazine written for the well-informed nonspecialist.

Harvard Business Review. 1922–. (Bimonthly)
Scholarly research articles dominate this journal that nevertheless covers the full range of business activity.

U.S. Office of Business Economics. *Survey of Current Business.* 1921–. (Monthly)
Provides descriptive and statistical information on income and trade. See a librarian for help in finding and using this title.

Wasserman, Paul, ed. *Encyclopedia of Business Information Sources.* 2 vols. Detroit: Gale, 1970.
This collection lists sources of information about business.

CHEMISTRY (SEE ALSO SCIENCE, GENERAL)

Bottle, Robert T. *The Use of Chemical Literature.* Hamden, Conn.: Archon Books, 1969.
Tells you how to use periodicals, abstracts, and other reference works dealing with chemistry.

Chemical Abstracts. 1907–. (Weekly)
This most comprehensible abstract journal is essential to the field; it is well worth the time necessary to learn how to use it. Check the semiannual index first.

Hemple, Clifford A., and G. G. Hawley. *The Encyclopedia of Chemistry.* New York: Van Nostrand Reinhold, 1973.
For students and nonscientists, it explains key ideas and terms.

Miall, Laurence M., and D. W. A. Sharp. *A New Dictionary of Chemistry.* New York: Wiley, 1968.
Includes biographical information on famous chemists as well as chemical terms.

COMPUTER SCIENCE

Business Automation. 1959–. (Monthly)
A particularized but important journal for those interested in computer applications.

Computer Abstracts. 1960–. (Monthly)
Published in England, this service includes books, articles, and conference reports. Very useful timesaver. See *Computing Reviews* below.

Computing Reviews. 1960–. (Monthly)
Published in the United States, this service includes both abstracts of research articles and critical reviews. Use along with *Computer Abstracts* above.

Datamation. 1957–. (Semimonthly)
Good for both specialists and general students, *Datamation* covers subjects as broad as the economics of computers and as narrow as limited technical details.

Microcomputer Index. 1980–. (Bimonthly)
Also available on-line.

PC. 1982–. (Semimonthly)
A popular magazine on IBM computers, including simplified discussions of technical subjects.

Pritchard, Alan. *A Guide to Computer Literature.* Hamden, Conn.: Linnet Books, 1972.
A descriptive list of sources, this book tells what is useful and where to find it.

CRIMINOLOGY (SEE ALSO SOCIAL SCIENCE AND SOCIOLOGY)

American Journal of Criminal Law. 1972–. (Three issues yearly)
This journal covers cases and analyzes social causes and significances. Primarily for the specialist.

Criminal Justice Abstracts. 1970–. (Quarterly)
Arranged by general subject with a detailed index as well, it covers a wide range of sources and subjects in the field.

Criminal Justice Periodicals Index. 1975–. (Three issues yearly)
Covering about 90 titles in criminology, criminal law, police, security, and related fields, this index is useful when used with *Criminal Justice Abstracts.*

ECONOMICS (SEE ALSO BUSINESS AND SOCIAL SCIENCE)

Fletcher, John, ed. *The Use of Economics Literature.* Hamden, Conn.: Archon Books, 1971.
Tells you how to use materials in the various branches of economics.

International Bibliography of Economics. 1955–. (Annual)
Another UNESCO-sponsored publication, this is an extensive listing of official and private writings in the field.

McGraw-Hill Dictionary of Modern Economics: A Handbook of Terms and Organizations. New York: McGraw-Hill, 1983.
For the nonspecialist, it defines about 1,400 terms in economics.

EDUCATION (SEE ALSO SOCIAL SCIENCE)

Current Index to Journals in Education. 1969–. (Monthly)
Includes a greater number of titles than *Education Index,* and a few articles are abstracted.

Education Index. 1929–. (Monthly)
Indexes educational periodicals and other publications by subject. Check the annual cumulations first.

Foskett, D. J. *How to Find Out: Educational Research.* New York: Pergamon Press, 1965.
Explains the kinds of educational publications and how to use them.

ENERGY STUDIES

Energy Daily. 1973–. (Weekly)
A newsletter that offers useful analysis of the most recent events dealing with energy, its development, and its uses.

Energy Index. 1971–. (Annual)
More than just an index, it includes reviews, statistics, analysis of legislation, and lists of films and conferences. Especially useful by itself as a source for research papers.

Energy Information Abstracts. 1976–. (Monthly)
Covers all types of energy resources, approaches, and sources. Easy to use.

ENGINEERING (SEE ALSO SCIENCE, GENERAL)

Engineering Index Monthly. 1901–. (Monthly)
Covers all aspects of engineering. Check the large annual volumes first for the subjects you want.

Jones, Franklin D., and Paul B. Schubert. *Engineering Encyclopedia.* New York: Industrial Press, 1963.
Defines engineering terms and provides brief analytical or historical articles in about 4,500 subjects.

Persons, Stanley A. J. *How to Find Out About Engineering.* Oxford: Pergamon Press, 1972.
A useful guide to all sorts of information in engineering. A good starting point.

Potter, J. H. *Handbook of the Engineering Sciences.* 2 vols. Princeton, N.J.: Van Nostrand, 1967.
Digests the principal engineering practices and provides explanations, calculations, and examples. Vol. 1 gives basic background in the sciences; vol. 2, the applications.

ENGINEERING, CIVIL

ASCE Publications Information. 1966–. (Bimonthly)
Indexes more than 30 journals of the American Society of Civil Engineers; annually provides about 1,600 abstracts on every aspect of the subject.

ENGINEERING, ELECTRICAL

Institute of Electrical and Electronics Engineers. *IEEE Standard Dictionary of Electrical and Electronics Terms.* 2nd ed. New York: Wiley-Interscience, 1977.
A standard reference for electrical engineering, it defines about 20,000 terms.

Science Abstracts: Series B, Electrical and Electronics Abstracts. 1898–. (Monthly)
Currently includes about 2,000 abstracts a month. Check the cumulative indexes first.

Shiers, George. *Bibliography of the History of Electronics.* Metuchen, N.J.: Scarecrow Press, 1972.
Covers historical development of electronics and communications.

ENGINEERING, NUCLEAR

Glasstone, Samuel. *Sourcebook on Atomic Energy.* Princeton, N.J.: Van Nostrand, 1967.
A standard basic reference book for beginning students and laymen.

International Atomic Energy Agency. *List of Bibliographies on Nuclear Energy.* 1960–.
Of some use if you're interested in international aspects of atomic power.

U.S. Atomic Energy Commission. *Nuclear Science Abstracts.* 1948–. (Semimonthly)
Covers official unclassified reports and studies. Usually very technical.

ENGLISH (SEE ALSO THEATER)

Altick, Richard D., and Andrew Wright. *Selective Bibliography for the Study of English and American Literature.* 6th ed. New York: Macmillan, 1978.
Especially good for its listing of key articles and useful works for the student.

Blanck, Jacob N., ed. *Bibliography of American Literature.* New Haven: Yale Univ. Press.
This multivolume series is a basic source including works by and about significant American writers.

Book Review Digest. 1905–. (Monthly)
Lists reviews of books published in the United States and reviewed in general magazines. Use with the next entry.

Book Review Index. 1965–. (Bimonthly)
Indexes reviews in 200 publications of fiction, nonfiction, humanities, and social science.

Buchanan-Brown, John, ed. *Cassell's Encyclopedia of World Literature.* New rev. ed. New York: Morrow, 1973.
A basic source for the field.

Holman, C. Hugh, and William Harmon. *A Handbook to Literature.* New York: Macmillan, 1986.
The most useful one-volume collection of terms, concepts, and movements in literature.

Modern Language Association. *MLA International Bibliography of Books and Articles on the Modern Languages and Literatures.* 1921–. (Annual)
An extensive listing, the *MLA Bibliography* is good for finding out what has been written about a book or author in any one year. Also lists bibliographies. (See also Chapter 3 for a sample entry and further discussion of this major bibliography in language and literature.)

The New Cambridge Bibliography of English Literature. 5 vols. Cambridge: Cambridge Univ. Press, 1969–75.
This is the standard work on English literature. Its five volumes cover major and minor figures with works by and about them.

Preminger, Alex, ed. *Princeton Encyclopedia of Poetry and Poetics.* Princeton: Princeton Univ. Press, 1974.
Over 1,000 articles on the history, theory, technique, and criticism of poetry.

Spiller, Robert E. *Literary History of the United States.* New York: Macmillan, 1974.

This comprehensive and sensible history covers the periods from the colonial days to the present and includes bibliographical information.

Wilson, F. P., Bonamy Dobree, and Norman Davis, gen. eds. *The Oxford History of English Literature.* New York: Oxford Univ. Press, 1945–.
The history is planned for 12 parts in 15 volumes, of which 11 have been published to date. Primarily concerned with English literature, this detailed history also covers politics, philosophy, scientific thought, and social movements related to the literature.

ENVIRONMENTAL STUDIES

Environmental Abstracts. 1971–. (Monthly)
An abstract service covering both published and media materials. A cumulative index is published as *Environment Index.*

Sarnoff, Paul. *The New York Times Encyclopedic Dictionary of the Environment.* New York: Quadrangle Books, 1971.
Defines 2,000 terms from environmental studies and problems.

Winton, Harry N. M. *Man and the Environment: A Bibliography of Selected Publications.* New York: Unipub, 1972.
Though now somewhat outdated, this basic source includes more than 1,200 entries.

FILM

Film Literature Index. 1973–. (Quarterly)
Covers periodical literature about film.

Manchel, Frank. *Film Study: A Resource Guide.* Rutherford, N.J.: Fairleigh Dickinson Univ. Press, 1973.
With its analysis of books and articles, it makes a good starting point.

GEOGRAPHY (SEE ALSO SOCIAL SCIENCE)

Brewer, J. Gordon. *The Literature of Geography: A Guide to Its Organisation and Use.* London: Linnet Books, 1978.
Helps you to the literature and techniques of geographical study.

Current Geographical Publications. 1938–. (Monthly)
An index to significant publications on geography.

Durrenberger, Robert W. *Geographical Research and Writing.* New York: Crowell, 1971.
This book guides you to the best sources of geographical information.

Schmieder, Allen A. *A Dictionary of Basic Geography.* Boston: Allyn and Bacon, 1970.
This listing of terms from political, economic, and cultural geography is aimed at the beginning student.

GEOLOGY

Bibliography and Index of Geology. 1933–. (Monthly)
In 1969 it began including articles on North American geology. For earlier years, see *Bibliography of North American Geology,* published annually from 1931 to 1970 by the Government Printing Office.

Gray, Margaret, and others. *Glossary of Geology.* Washington, D.C.: American Geological Institute, 1977.
A useful listing of terms found in geological literature.

Ward, Dederick C., and Marjorie W. Wheeler. *Geologic Reference Sources.* Metuchen, N.J.: Scarecrow Press, 1981.
For both student and specialist, this guide provides useful bibliographical leads.

HISTORY (SEE ALSO SOCIAL SCIENCE)

American Historical Association. *Guide to Historical Literature.* New York: Macmillan, 1961.
A standard resource for history; go here first.

Facts on File: A Weekly News Digest. 1940–.
Good for events since 1940 under such categories as national affairs, economy, science, and others.

Historical Abstracts, 1775–1945. 1955–. (Quarterly)
Includes U.S. history until 1964 volume. For later U.S. historical writing, see the following entry.

HISTORY, AMERICAN

America: History and Life. A Guide to Periodical Literature. 1954–. (Quarterly)
Covers U.S. and Canadian histories. Divided into parts: (A) articles and abstracts; (B) book reviews; (C) bibliography; (D) annual index.

Friedel, Frank, and Richard K. Showman, eds. *Harvard Guide to American History*. 2 vols. Cambridge, Mass.: Belknap Press of Harvard Univ. Press, 1974.
This is the reliable place to begin for finding information on U.S. history.

HOME ECONOMICS

Home Economics Research Journal. 1972–. (Quarterly)
Covers doctoral dissertations and master's theses in this field, along with articles reporting research.

Journal of Home Economics. 1909–. (Quarterly)
Deals primarily with what is being taught in high schools and colleges; sometimes helpful.

Education Index. 1929/30–. (Monthly)
Includes home economics topics among those it indexes.

MATHEMATICS

Karush, William. *The Crescent Dictionary of Mathematics*. New York: Macmillan, 1962.
A useful general work for beginning students.

Mathematical Reviews. 1940–. (Monthly)
These abstracts cover pure and applied mathematical literature. Usually detailed and demanding articles.

Parke, Nathan G. *Guide to the Literature of Mathematics and Physics*. New York: Dover, 1958.
A reliable, if somewhat dated, "how-to" book on the use of mathematical sources.

MUSIC

Duckles, Vincent H. *Music Reference and Research Materials: An Annotated Bibliography*. New York: Free Press, 1974.
This bibliography is the essential source for research in music.

High Fidelity. 1951–. (Monthly)
This general magazine has authoritative articles on musicians and their music as well as on audio equipment.

Music Index: The Key to Current Music Periodical Literature. 1949–.
Indexed by author and subject, the *Music Index* covers most of the field; it is especially good for recent music trends.

Music Journal: Educational Music Magazine. 1943–. (Bimonthly)
An excellent source on contemporary music; often controversial.

NURSING

Cumulative Index to Nursing and Allied Health Literature. 1961–. (Bimonthly)
This index covers all significant English-language nursing journals and some medical journals.

Facts About Nursing. New York: American Nurses' Association, 1935–.
An annual publication, this volume includes detailed information about nursing as a profession.

International Nursing Index. 1966–. (Quarterly)
Worldwide coverage of nursing journals and medical literature dealing with nursing. It supplements the *Cumulative Index.*

Stewart, Isabel M., and Anne L. Austin. *A History of Nursing from Ancient to Modern Times.* New York: Putnam, 1962.
An introductory history of nursing, it includes useful bibliographies.

PHILOSOPHY

Borchardt, Dietrich Hans. *How to Find Out in Philosophy.* Oxford: Pergamon Press, 1968.
A helpful guide for the layman or beginning student.

Edwards, Paul, ed. *Encyclopedia of Philosophy.* 8 vols. New York: Macmillan, 1967.
This source has long and substantial articles covering all aspects of philosophy, including Eastern thought.

Journal of Philosophy. 1904–. (Monthly)
Though often difficult reading, this journal also has useful historical articles and some dealing with the philosophy of science.

Journal of the History of Philosophy. 1963–. (Quarterly)
As the title indicates, this journal deals with the development of philosophic thought, almost exclusively Western thought.

The Philosopher's Index. 1967–. (Quarterly)
Abstracts articles in about 150 journals, with many technical discussions.

PHYSICS (SEE ALSO SCIENCE, GENERAL)

Condon, Edward U., and Hugh Odishaw. *Handbook of Physics.* New York: McGraw-Hill, 1967.

An encyclopedic handbook with chapters by specialists; covers subjects ranging from the mechanics of particles, to thermodynamics, to nuclear physics. Includes bibliographies.

Current Physics Index. 1975–. (Quarterly)
Provides access to journals and conferences published by the American Institute of Physics; covers most American and much Soviet literature on physics, usually in highly technical language.

Parke, Nathan G. *Guide to the Literature of Mathematics and Physics.* New York: Dover, 1958.
Reliable, but somewhat outdated, this book tells you how to use sources in mathematics and physics.

Science Abstracts, Series A, Physics Abstracts. 1898–. (Bimonthly)
With about 85,000 entries annually, this series provides comprehensive coverage of the technical literature of physics. Check the cumulative indexes first.

Thewlis, James. *Concise Dictionary of Physics and Related Subjects.* Oxford: Pergamon Press, 1973.
Defines terms in physics and other fields of related study.

POLITICAL SCIENCE (SEE ALSO SOCIAL SCIENCE)

American Political Science Review. 1906–. (Quarterly)
The basic journal in the discipline, it deals with government, administration, political theory, and international law.

CIS Index. 1969–. (Monthly)
This Congressional Information Service index covers nearly all documents published by the U.S. Congress. Comprehensive indexing makes this a very useful source on current governmental actions.

Facts on File, A Weekly News Digest. 1940–.
This series is especially good for events since 1940, listed under such categories as national affairs, economy, and sciences, among others.

Foreign Affairs. 1922–. (Quarterly)
Generally considered the most prestigious journal in the field, it often has some of the current governmental officials among its contributors.

Holler, Frederick L. *The Information Sources of Political Science.* 5 vols. Santa Barbara, Calif.: ABC-Clio, 1975.
This source will guide you to finding out what you need. Its annotations are especially helpful.

International Bibliography of Political Science. 1952–. (Annual)
Sponsored by UNESCO, this is one of the basic sources to check in
your search.

PSYCHOLOGY (SEE ALSO SOCIAL SCIENCE)

Bell, James E. *A Guide to Library Research in Psychology.* Dubuque,
Iowa: W. C. Brown, 1971.
Tells you where to find sources of information.

Eysenck, H. J., and others. *Encyclopedia of Psychology.* London: Search
Press, 1972.
Includes lengthy articles and short definitions covering important
terms and concepts in psychology. Good bibliographical help.

Harriman, Philip L. *Handbook of Psychological Terms.* Totowa, N.J.: Lit-
tlefield, Adams, 1965.
With reasonably clear definitions, this is a reliable guide for beginning research.

The Harvard List of Books in Psychology. Cambridge, Mass.: Harvard
Univ. Press, 1971.
An annotated guide to more than 700 titles in psychology, this
source saves you time in finding information.

Journal of Applied Psychology. 1917–. (Quarterly)
Covers all areas of applied psychology except clinical treatment. Often deals with social behavior, leadership qualities, and practical industrial matters.

Psychological Abstracts. 1927–. (Monthly)
Includes new books, articles, and technical literature. Be sure to
check the Cumulated Subject Indexes to save time.

Psychology Today. 1967–. (Monthly)
Almost a general-interest magazine; however, it covers the field in
language most students can understand and does so reliably. A basic
source for beginning researchers.

RELIGION

Adams, Charles J., ed. *A Reader's Guide to the Great Religions.* New
York: Free Press, 1965.
A bibliographic guide to both Eastern and Western religions, this
book helps you find more sources of information.

The Catholic Periodical and Literature Index. 1930–. (Bimonthly)
Covers 129 periodicals of Catholic origin, including many published
outside the United States.

Hastings, James, ed. *Encyclopedia of Religion and Ethics.* 12 vols. New York: Scribner, 1908–27.
Comprehensive, it includes articles on nearly every religion and related subjects like customs, religious folklore, and psychology.

History of Religions. 1961–. (Quarterly)
Highly scholarly, this journal is nevertheless useful for any beginning researcher interested in the subject.

Mitros, Joseph F. *Religions: A Select, Classified Bibliography.* New York: Learned Publications, 1973.
A classified bibliography especially useful for students.

Religious and Theological Abstracts. 1958–. (Quarterly)
Nonsectarian, it covers Christian, Jewish, and Muslim publications.

Theology Today. 1944–. (Quarterly)
An intellectual journal, this product of the Princeton Theological Seminary often deals with current controversy in theology.

SCIENCE, GENERAL

Applied Science and Technology Index. 1913–. (Monthly)
This index covers publications in aeronautics and astronautics, chemistry, construction, earth sciences, physics, and other fields.

Grogan, Denis Joseph. *Science and Technology: An Introduction to the Literature.* Hamden, Conn.: Linnet Books, 1973.
Tells you how to find information in scientific publications.

McGraw-Hill Encyclopedia of Science and Technology. 15 vols. New York: McGraw-Hill, 1982.
In more detail, perhaps, than you can use, it covers all branches of science. It is a good starting place for a general science topic.

SOCIAL SCIENCE

Journal of Social Issues. 1944–. (Quarterly)
Especially good for the nonspecialist, this journal analyzes current social problems in language intended for a general audience.

London Bibliography of the Social Sciences. 1931–.
The most extensive bibliography in this very broad field; use it as a guide if you have a specific subject.

Public Affairs Information Service. 1915–. (Semimonthly)
Indexes current publications about economics and social conditions besides the general category of public affairs. (See Chapter 3 for a sample entry and further discussion of this index.)

White, Carl M. *Sources of Information in the Social Sciences*. Chicago: American Library Association, 1973.
This is the standard guide to finding out where to go for information; it includes a bibliographic guide to these fields: history, geography, economics, business administration, sociology, anthropology, psychology, education, and political science.

SOCIOLOGY (SEE ALSO SOCIAL SCIENCE)

Gould, Julius, and William L. Kolb, eds. *A Dictionary of the Social Sciences*. New York: Free Press, 1964.
Special emphasis on sociology; includes bibliographical references.

International Bibliography of Sociology. 1952–.
Sponsored by UNESCO, this is one of the most useful guides in this broad field.

Sociological Abstracts. 1953–. (5/Year)
A classified listing of abstracts, this service can help you find out recent research results.

Sociological Inquiry. 1930–. (Quarterly)
An authoritative, scholarly journal that students can use, it deals with current developments and carries general articles.

Sociology and Social Research. 1916–. (Quarterly)
Reports on research on current problems in the United States and many foreign countries; usually includes at least one historical article.

THEATER (SEE ALSO ENGLISH)

Brockett, Oscar G., and others. *A Bibliographical Guide to Research in Speech and Dramatic Arts*. Chicago: Scott, Foresman, 1963.
Especially useful for students, it has some annotations to guide you in selecting sources.

Drama Review. 1955–. (Quarterly)
The leading periodical on the subject, especially new trends in contemporary theater.

Educational Theatre Journal. 1949–. (Quarterly)
This journal of the American Theatre Association is designed for college-level theater and focuses on theatrical history, theory, and criticism.

Hartnoll, Phyllis. *The Oxford Companion to the Theatre.* London: Oxford Univ. Press, 1983.
Covers all periods of theater (to 1964) but does not include movies. Useful for explaining terms and identifying actors or characters.

New York Theatre Critics Review. 1940–. (30 issues yearly)
This collection provides reviews from major New York newspapers and national magazines. Useful for comparing critics' responses to a production.

Variety. 1905–. (Weekly)
The basic paper of the entertainment world, it includes theater reviews as well as background material and news from all parts of show business.

Theatre/Drama Abstracts. 1974–. (Three issues yearly)
Provides abstracts and indexes to more than 100 international journals dealing with speech, plays, reviews, and scripts.

Index